NAMES
ACROSS
NIAGARA

Vanwell Publishing Limited

St. Catharines, Ontario

NAMES ACROSS NIAGARA

John N. Jackson

Assisted by Sheila M. Wilson

Historical Review: John Burtniak
Toponymic Review: Michael B. Smart

Vanwell Publishing Limited

St. Catharines, Ontario

Canadian Cataloguing in Publication Data

Jackson, John N., 1925-
          Names Across Niagara
(Niagara heritage series)
Bibliography: p.
Includes index.
ISBN 0-920277-26-8

1.   Names, Geographical - Ontario - Niagara
Peninsula.   2. Niagara Peninsula (Ont.) - History,
Local.   I. Title.

FC3095.N5J32 1989   971.3'38   C89-094431-8
F1059.N5J32 1989

Design Susan Nicholson
Cover   Mark Waters
Maps   Loris Gasparotto

Vanwell Publishing Limited
1 Northrup Cres.
P.O. Box 2131, Stn. B
St. Catharines, ON
L2M 6P5

CONTENTS

MAPS AND TABLES

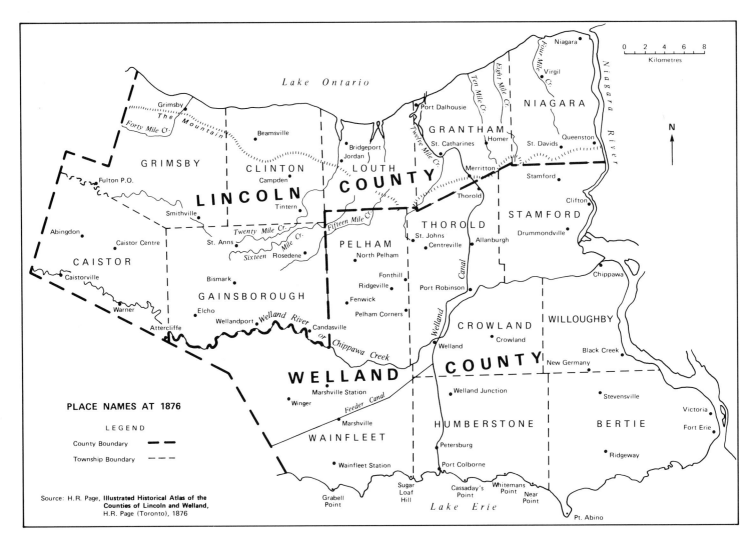

PLACE NAMES AT 1876

LEGEND

County Boundary — — —

Township Boundary - - -

Source: H.R. Page, **Illustrated Historical Atlas of the
Counties of Lincoln and Welland,**
H.R. Page (Toronto), 1876

Fig. 1

Introduction

THE STUDY OF NAMES

Names as a reminder of past circumstances and traditions in the landscape are one of the cultural factors that give meaning, purpose, character and individuality to place (Fig. 1). They also provide an opportunity for recognition of past names and circumstances when creating new ones. The study of place names, derived from "toponym" as a name for a place, is called "toponymy", and the more comprehensive study of area names is "choronymy". These studies are linguistic when origins are involved, statistical when data bases have to be developed, and administrative when decisions are made to approve, change or add names.

The many activities of government, descriptions of property, and documents involving legal rights require uniformity and unambiguity. Names must be scribed on maps in a consistent form as an essential part of the cartographic art. They appear on buildings, streets are named, and signs indicate the names of towns and villages. Bilingualism presents the acute problems of translation, and the persistent reminder that names must be perceived and treated officially as "names", not simply as "words".

Though a name is used frequently and continuously, its antecedents are often lost or blurred by the mists of time. There may be alternative spellings or meanings, and controversy may exist over the precise origin, but each name is a heritage endowment. Names provide a sense of appreciation and an understanding for the personality of place, and it is this search for explanation which provides the major theme of this book.

The approach for this study is geographical and spatial. Also, as literally thousands of names exist at Niagara, it is selective rather than comprehensive. It would be an impossible task to deal with all names in one volume. This book covers the names of counties, townships and most of the settlements that have arisen within this administrative matrix. It includes the physical features of rivers, lakes, shorelines, relief and vegetation. It extends into a selection of streets, subdivisions and the buildings that together create our complex modern environment. The names of vessels that ply our waters, transportation networks, and names arising from industrial, commercial and business activities are also explored.

There is romance in naming **Homer** after the greatest of Greek poets. There is hope for the future in naming **Jordan** after the Promised Land. There is personal preference by Lieutenant Governor Simcoe when he imposed English place names from a country more familiar to himself than to the settlers. The independent spirit of displaced loyalists is apparent by the rejection of **Newark** and the revival of the name **Niagara** for the first major settlement; also, the **Grand River** never became the **Ouse** as required by Simcoe. Old wars and days of glory can be conjured up in place names such as **Queenston Heights** or **Lundy's Lane. Dick's Creek,** named after a pioneer in Butler's Rangers, has become a permanent part of the canal scene in St. Catharines. The whole gamut of human experience is conveyed through the names we give to places, imprints of each successive age.

THE NAMING PROCESS

The Niagara Peninsula has progressed through several phases of settlement evolution, with each leaving its mark on names in the landscape. The several elements in the physical background had each to be named, a process that begins with names of Amerindian and French origin. Later periods include an Early Colonial or Pioneer period from the 1780s to the 1820s, amended considerably by a Late Colonial Phase of expansion which included the foundation era of the Welland Canal. More recent epochs include a Railway-Industrial Period to the mid-1920s, and thereafter an Automobile Era which becomes especially pervasive after World War II. Names provide a cumulative expression in the landscape. As new names are added, the old either survives, or is amended or replaced by later generations.

When tracing the origin and spelling of a place name, the earliest documents should be examined but even so, many phonetic spellings may exist and the explanation of meaning must often be an interpretation. **Lake Erie, Lake Ontario** and **Niagara** are in this category. Often, two or more possibilities of meaning exist, as for **Queenston, Winona** or **White Pigeon.** The possessive "**s**" creates problems: **St. David** or **St. David's?**

Every geographical name has a story to tell. But a word of warning. It is not always wise to accept a name at its face value. For example, **Stoney Creek** (not Stony, an earlier usage), where a rocky stream falls from the Niagara Escarpment, would seem to be a descriptive name. But, as an early settler named Edmund Stoney lived there and kept a store or trading post, the name could be after the creek, the settler, or both. Do names such as **Green** and **Black** refer to a person or a colour? Which individual is recalled when a Christian name is used?

At some future date it is possible that **Lake Gibson** in Thorold might be confused with Dr. James Gibson, the first President of nearby Brock University, but the name refers to a hydro official. **Stonebridge,** an early name for Humberstone, was not a bridge across the Welland Canal, but where stones set in a creek provided a passage. Pitfalls always exist for the student of place names.

The difficulties of the naming process, and the need for consistency and accuracy on maps, led to the creation of the **Geographic Board of Canada** in 1897, changed to the **Canadian Board of Geographic Names** in 1948, and since 1961 the **Canadian Permanent Committee on Geographic Names.** The officially approved or "correct" spelling of each name is listed in the **Gazetteer of Canada,** published by the federal government separately for each province, a process that began only in 1952 with the publication of data for Southwest Ontario. Updated in 1962 and 1974, the latest edition was prepared in 1988 by the Canadian Permanent Committee on Geographic Names.

Names are not duplicated within a municipality, but many street names are common to communities throughout Niagara, for example **King, Queen, Main, Orchard** and **Church.** The issue of non-repetition across the regional landscape arose in 1988, when St. Catharines named a street **Sawmill Road.** The Mayor of Pelham challenged this, as it duplicated a road name in his municipality. In 1988 he suggested that all Niagara municipalities should submit their street name proposals to a central body to avoid duplication. This issue could become more serious with the implementation of a regional emergency telephone system, whereby only a caller's street address appears on the dispatcher's terminal to identify the call's location.

Serious retrospective thought is required when changes or additions to local names are required. They become part of the personality of place, the 'who', 'why' and 'what' behind the image and facts of landscape from which we might derive certain ideas and details of past circumstances. The search for this understanding is not easy. The ensuing narrative will provide examples of good and bad, the exciting and the mundane, the rational and the irrational in the names that provide meaning and character to the human and physical landscapes of the Niagara Peninsula.

"Let no man say there is nothing in names, for they run the whole gamut of human interest." Louis Blake Duff

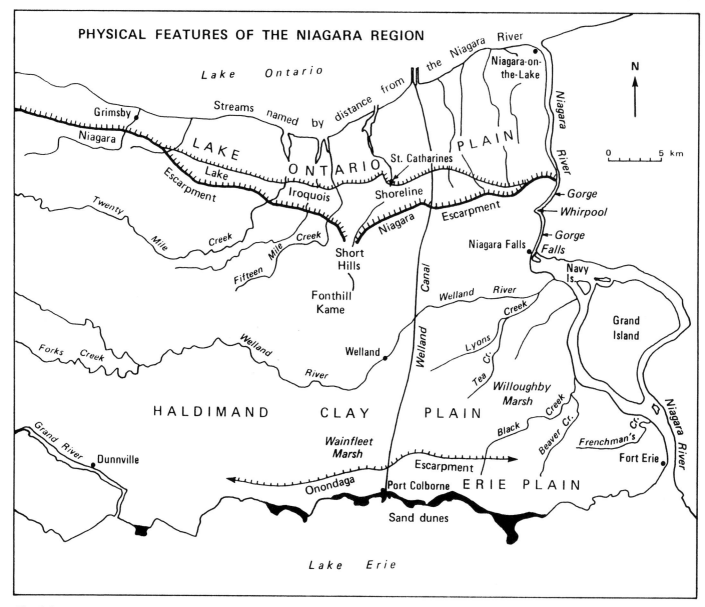

Fig. 1.1

1.

The Physical Background

Because the physical framework of water and land has strongly influenced the location, form and growth of human activities, naming the natural background presents an important and now instructive part of the naming process (Fig. 1.1). The rivers and lakeshores provided the first awareness of terrain for travellers, for pioneer routes of entry, sites of potential water power suitable for mills, and harbours on the lake fronts. The Niagara River and the internal streams had to be crossed by bridges. The qualities of soil, climate and vegetation attracted the pioneer more to the north than to the south of the Peninsula; the frequency and size of communities, the production of farms and the emergence of the famed Niagara Fruit Belt reflect such differences. Industry has taken advantage of mineral and agricultural resources. Transportation routes, from early roads through canals and railways to modern highways, have logically been aligned along the easiest route to follow and construct.

A range of terms has been used to describe the many features of land and water that create Niagara's landscapes. An elevated area of land may be referred to as **Bank, Escarpment, Heights, Hill, Kame, Lookout, Moraine, Mount, Mountain** or **Ridge.** The opposite, low-lying land, may be named **Bog, Dale, Flats, Glen, Gorge, Hollow, Marsh, Plain, Ravine, Swamp, Vale** or **Valley.** Some of these names such as Bog, Marsh and Swamp are synonymous; others have subtle differences of meaning, including the distinction between Ridge and Escarpment or Kame and Moraine, that involve complex studies in physical geography. In total, they express the rich diversity of landforms that occur in the Peninsula.

THE NIAGARA PENINSULA

A "Peninsula" is a neck of land almost surrounded by water. Saanich, B.C. and Nova Scotia are peninsulas, but not Niagara. Regional, provincial and federal maps perpetuate this false impression for they terminate their detail at the boundary, leaving the other side blank. Niagara is a peninsula only in administrative and political terms. Physically, it thrusts into and is a continuity with New York State, to which it is directly and visibly connected by several highway and railway bridges, many journeys of passage over these inter-connecting links, and by hydro-electric cables and pipelines.

Like Avalon, Newfoundland, or Chignecto, Nova Scotia, Niagara is an "Isthmus". As recorded by an early map-maker before separation from the United States, it is "l'Isthme qui sépare les Lacs Erié et Ontario." Current geographical literature refers to the Niagara Peninsula as a "Land Bridge" or "Land Corridor" between Lakes Ontario and Erie, a characteristic that has resulted in the routing of communications between the Detroit and the Niagara River Frontiers, and strong penetration of the regional economy from the United States. It is a "Gateway" to and from Southern Ontario. **The Corridor**, a newsletter published by the Niagara Regional Development Corporation, is a title that captures the essence of this regional situation.

The **Niagara Peninsula** is bounded by Lake Ontario to the north, the Niagara River to the east, and Lake Erie to the south. The inland boundary to the west, though imprecise, is generally deemed to include the Niagara Fruit Belt and to exclude Hamilton. The lower length of the Grand River provides a convenient boundary in the southwest, for here a dam diverted water to supply the Welland Canal and Dunnville arose as a canal town at this dam.

Geographically, the Niagara Peninsula is larger in extent than the **Niagara Region,** a defined administrative unit of local government within specific boundaries (Fig. 3.3). Locally, Port Dalhousie is referred to as "The Peninsula within the Peninsula". It sits at the end of a promontory between Lake Ontario and Martindale Pond, and is sharply defined by these water boundaries.

THE LAKE FRONTAGES

West from the Niagara River, the creeks that enter Lake Ontario are named approximate with the distance of their mouths in miles from the entrance to the Niagara River. The correct title is, for example, **Twenty Mile Creek,** not Twenty-Mile, 20 Mile, nor 20-Mile Creek. **The Twenty** and **The Fifteen** are terms still in use, as in a senior citizens' **Club of the Twenty.** Metric conversion, adopted as Canadian policy in 1971, has not yet enforced a change!

The numbering of creeks east and west from the Niagara River is testimony to the great importance of the Niagara River and the associated Niagara Portage as the major route of entry from the Atlantic Ocean to the inland heart of the North American continent. Whether it be creeks entering Lake Ontario, or headlands projecting into Lake Erie, both provided some form of security for the craft of early explorers, fur traders, missionaries, and soldiers. Shallow-draught vessels on Lake Ontario could be manoeuvred into the protection of creeks with steep banks, and vessels on Lake Erie might seek shelter from prevailing westerly winds in the lee of headlands.

The creeks along Lake Ontario, impounded behind lakeshore sand bars, have ponds numbered **Two, Four, Eight, Fifteen, Sixteen,** and **Eighteen. Twelve** and **Twenty Mile Ponds** have received names: **Martindale Pond** on Twelve Mile Creek, created by a weir on the Second Welland Canal, is now home to the international **Royal Canadian Henley Regatta** as a highlight of the summer sports season in St. Catharines; the name **Jordan Harbour** persists for the pond of Twenty Mile Creek, though the "harbour" status has been obsolete since a railway bridge prevented upstream navigation.

Four and **Fifty Mile Points** are numbered after their respective creeks; **McNab Point** is after the original proprietors, McNabb, but written McNab and perhaps MacNab. The Burlington area is known popularly as **Head-of-the-Lake,** from the earlier **Fond du Lac** of the French. Beaches are infrequent along the shore of Lake Ontario, though **Burlington Beach, Grimsby Beach, Michigan** and **Jones Beach** in St. Catharines, provide exceptions.

With a contrasting physical environment of rocky headlands and sandy bays but no significant inflowing creeks, a different type of nomenclature prevails along the shoreline of Lake Erie. Points named after the families of early settlers include **Cassaday, Grabell, Morgans, Near, Rathfon, Reebs, Sherkston, Shisler** and **Whiteman. Windmill Point** is a functional name of obvious pioneer connotation.

The Sugar Loaf, a large conical mass as seen from the lake was so recognized and described in a trader's diary of 1765. During the War of 1812 this hill became part of a semaphore signalling system on the high points of land that

A combination of location (Grimsby) and a physical attribute (beach) introduces this popular Lake Ontario resort.

extended across the Niagara Peninsula. Instead of the one apt descriptive name, the **Gazetteer of Canada** now distinguishes between **Sugar Loaf Point** and **Sugarloaf Hill.** To have different official spellings for parts of the same feature, **Sugar Loaf** and the elided **Sugarloaf,** is unacceptable.

The bays and beaches in the vicinity are often named after an observed physical characteristic: **Bay Beach, Cedar Bay, Crescent Beach, Crystal Beach, Gravel Bay, Gravelly Bay, Long Beach, Low Banks, Pleasant Beach, Silver Bay** and **Willow Bay.** The contrast of a company name is used when the locality has been used for industrial purposes, as at **Empire Beach,** Sherkston, after the Empire Limestone Co., and **Nickel Beach,** Port Colborne, after the International Nickel Company (INCO Limited).

THE ESCARPMENT AND PLAINS

The Peninsula's major internal relief feature, the linear rock outcrop inland from Lake Ontario, is an escarpment slope now generally referred to as the **Niagara Escarpment,** which is geological terminology. Named **Mount Dorchester** in 1792 after Lord Dorchester, the Governor General, by Lieutenant Governor Simcoe, it was typically referred to as **The Edge** or **The Mountain** in early accounts, with "mountain" being merited hyperbole for abrupt slopes rather than for the height involved.

Mountain and **Ridge Roads** either follow its length or cross the brow between Queenston Heights and Grimsby. **Rockway (Rockway Falls)** is a self-explanatory descriptive name, Rockway Falls previously being **Roland's Falls** after the Roland family. **Queenston Heights** and **Burlington Heights** tower above their respective communities. The **Bruce Trail,** named because it follows the Niagara Escarpment to the Bruce Peninsula on Lake Huron and Georgian Bay, weaves its distinctive hiking route along the crest from Queenston Heights to Tobermory.

A secondary and lower ridge running inland from Lake Erie, is called the **Onondaga Escarpment,** also geological terminology. It supports the village of **Ridgeway,** and the **Ridgewood** subdivision. **Ridge, Ridgemount** and **Ridgeway Roads** follow this ridge. **The Fonthill Kame,** the highest ground in the Peninsula and another geological expression, refers to a deposit of sand and gravel created during the melting of glacial ice. **Lookout Point** is suggestive of the height involved, and the ridgelike character is reflected in the name for the village of **Ridgeville.**

The **Short Hills,** a pioneer and very apt term for the broken terrain to the north, is an area with many low or

Shoreline toponymy becomes a recreational endowment.

Ridgeville: A community name emphasizing its natural surroundings.

"short", flat topped hills broken by sharply incised valleys. The **Short Hills Provincial Park** occupies a part of this locality, which is a sand-filled embayment in the otherwise east-west continuity of the Niagara Escarpment. "Hill" is also used at **Drummond Hill,** Niagara Falls, for the raised land on which the Battle of Lundy's Lane was fought in 1814. **Pay's Hill,** after William Pay who became Superintendent of the Welland Railway in 1870, was also known as **Lock 2 Hill,** because of its location above this lock on the Second Welland Canal at **Welland Vale,** St. Catharines.

The Niagara Escarpment divides the Niagara Peninsula into two distinctive plains of flat or gently rolling terrain. The Power **Ontario Plain** is named after its proximity to this lake. The upper **Haldimand (Clay) Plain** is named after Haldimand County to the west, into which it extends. An alternative nomenclature, the **Welland-Tonawanda Plain,** reflects that the plain lies within the drainage area of these two rivers and also that it continues east of the Niagara River into New York State. Between the Onondaga Escarpment and Lake Erie, the slender **Erie Plain** is named because of its situation next to this lake.

THE NIAGARA RIVER

The **Niagara River,** is a narrow passage of water joining two larger bodies, is technically a "strait" and was so called in early accounts. It was considered, correctly, to be a component of the extensive, inland drainage system referred to as **The River of Canada** by both Jacques Cartier and Samuel de Champlain, and an integral part of the **St. Lawrence** system of interconnected lakes and rivers that extends from Lake Superior to Quebec City. This continuity was referred to as the **St. Lawrence** in early accounts, an uninterrupted succession later broken into sections which at Niagara include the Niagara River, and Lakes Erie and Ontario. Of interest with respect to this physical continuity is that a French map at the turn of the 18th century referred to the Upper Niagara River from Lake Erie to the falls as the **Rivière Erié (Erié).**

A return to the original St. Lawrence terminology for the total system occurred in 1951 when **The St. Lawrence Seaway Authority** was established for the purpose of constructing, maintaining and operating a deep waterway between the Upper Great Lakes and Montreal. The name St. Lawrence was then applied to the total length of the waterway, not just its length along the St. Lawrence River. The **St. Lawrence**, from the French **Saint Laurent** and its earlier orthographic variations, was named on 10 August 1535 in commemoration of the Saint whose feast day it was. Cartier gave the name to a bay on the north shore of the present-day **Gulf of St. Lawrence.** The term was gradually applied to the gulf then to the river, then inland to the upcountry system of rivers and lakes.

As befits the scenic quality of the landscape, much descriptive physical terminology occurs along the Niagara River. French terms were first used: **Debouchure,** a mouth or opening, for its point of departure from Lake Ontario; **Declivité,** a descending slope, for the rapids upstream from the falls; and **Les Chutes de Niagara, Ongiara Sault** and **Sault (Saut) de Niagara** for the falls themselves. It is unfortunate that these resonant terms are not still used, as to view a declivity, debouchure or a chute would be a distinctive tourist experience!

The falls have received several rapturous and ecstatic names, including the **Grand Falls of Niagara** by Lady Simcoe. She described the present American falls as the **Fort Schlosser Fall** and the **Montmorency Fall,** and referred to the **Great Horseshoe** on the Canadian side. To Father Louis Hennepin who saw the falls in 1678, they were an incredible **Cataract** and **Waterfall.** Today, **Horseshoe Falls,** named after its distinctive shape, has become a world-famous attraction. On the American bank are the **American** or **Rainbow Falls,** separated by **Luna Island** from the **Luna** or **Bridal Veil Falls.** Luna, from the Latin for moon, refers to the coloured "Lunar Bow" (as in rainbow) that could be seen when there was sufficient moonlight to illuminate the spray above the falls.

Scenery is not necessarily a fixed asset. A name may survive the destruction of a recognized place. For example, even though the flat overhang of **Table Rock** has collapsed, it remains **Table Rock House and Scenic Tunnels.** Another overhang, **The Star of the Great Eastern** at Niagara Glen, named after its visible resemblance to an early trans-Atlantic liner, has been pared for safety reasons.

Niagara Glen is also a name of interest. **Glen** is a Scottish (Gaelic) word for a steepsided narrow valley, with the implication of being both rugged and wild, and therefore a suitable term for use in this locale at Niagara. Coined by the Niagara Parks Commission when developing walks in this scenic locality, "Glen" is also used at **Power Glen,** where the penstocks of the DeCew Power Generating Station descend into the sharply incised valley of Twelve Mile Creek.

Within **Niagara Glen,** its rockfalls from the cliff above have resulted in individual names for its distinctively-shaped boulders. **Devil's Oven Pothole,** bored through rock by river action whirling loose stones, now provides a tubular passageway. Other revealing descriptive names are **Balancing Rock, Tree Top Rock, Leaning Rock** and **Indian Face.**

The **Whirlpool** and the **Whirlpool Rapids** have given rise to the **Whirlpool Golf Course** and **Whirlpool Road.** The **Spanish Aero Car,** named because of its promotion by Spanish businessmen, is a cableway that departs from **Thompson Point,** named after J. Enoch Thompson, the Spanish Consul at Toronto.

The falls have continued to recede through erosion. A former site was at the head of **Foster's Flats. Clifton,** and **Clifton Hill** with its cluster of amusement attractions where the magnificent **Clifton House Hotel** began its operation in 1835, are presumed to be named after Clifton on the gorge of the River Avon at Bristol, England.

As the international boundary follows not the mid-line of the Niagara River but the mid-point of the deepest channel so as not to dissect the mid-stream islands, only **Navy Island** of the major islands is Canadian territory. The name recalls a British shipyard established in 1763 at the southern end which produced sloops and schooners, the first vessels to navigate the Upper Great Lakes under the British flag. Navy Island also played an important role in the abortive Mackenzie Rebellion. Here in 1837 William Lyon Mackenzie

Glen, a Scottish Gaelic word for valley, imposed on the Canadian landscape.

proclaimed a Provisional Government for the State of Upper Canada, with himself as its first President.

Hogg Island, at the outlet from the Welland River where the Welland Canal Company in the late 1820s made the **Chippawa Cut,** severed land from the bank of the Niagara River. It is probably named after Thomas Hogg, an engineer on this project. A lesser possibility is a name derived from the logs floated down the Welland River, which were stored in "hog pens". Hogg Island was reduced in size when the Welland River was reversed and deepened in the late 1910s to serve as the intake system for the Chippawa-Queenston Power Canal.

FLORA, FAUNA AND CLIMATE

Landscape features are sometimes named after birds, animals trees and other flora present in that vicinity. Above the Horseshoe Falls, the goat herds of **Goat Island** and the gulls of **Gull Island** have been immortalized through the naming process. **Rattlesnake Ledge** at Niagara Glen is where timber rattlesnakes once lived, and the nearby

picnic area of **Wintergreen Flats** (the location of an earlier river bed), suggests a vegetational cover of year-round significance. **Wolf Creek** near Wellandport indicates the former presence of this animal.

Willowbank (Willow Bank), constructed in 1834, is the former home of the Hon. Alexander Hamilton, the son of Queenston's founder and Sheriff of Lincoln County; it was so named after a grove of willow trees flourishing between it and the Niagara River. A fine example of colonial architecture with wooden Ionic columns, the building has become the head office for wines bottled under a **Willowbank** label.

Grass Island Pool and the submerged **Grass Island Weir,** above the falls and rapids in the Niagara River, are presumably named after the vegetation of a former island. **Hawks Point**, Grimsby, is a local name for an area where these birds soar in rising air streams. **Beaver Dams** and **Beaver Creek** doubtless indicate the meadows, dams and ponds built by beaver which the early settlers encountered.

Fruit varieties acknowledged in the street names of St. Catharines and Niagara Falls include the **Elberta** peach and the **Concord** grape. **Fruitland, Vineland** and **Vinemount** depict major local products. **Nursery Lane,** Fonthill, is a reminder of once extensive nurseries, and **Deverardo Drive** of Dexter D'Everardo who planted many trees in the area. **Maple, Elm, Oak-Oakdale, Peach-Peachdale** and **Cherry** are common street names. Lincoln has a **Locust Lane,** probably after nearby locust (acacia) trees.

The **Niagara Fruit Belt,** a recognized term for an important area of tender fruit growing that produces the greater part of Canada's peaches, cherries and grapes, has become acceptable terminology for the area between Lake Ontario and the Niagara Escarpment, and its extensions south to the Fonthill Kame. The clash between extensive urban expansion and the high quality soils and climate of the **Tender Fruit Lands** has rivetted public attention on this primary natural resource and the need to safeguard its assets in perpetuity.

A local climatic detail is recalled in **Hurricane Road**

between Fonthill and Thorold, where a summer cyclone of 1792 devastated a swath of land. **Thunder Bay** on Lake Erie might recall another storm. The local climatic feature of a rainbow formed in the spray by the sun's rays has given rise to the **Rainbow Carillon, Rainbow Gardens** and **Rainbow Bridge** at Niagara Falls.

INTERNAL DRAINAGE

Places named after the numbered creeks in the north of the Peninsula were frequently renamed, probably because of confusion as the same creek often attracted a series of settlements to its crossing points and several mill sites might have developed along its length. The **Upper Four** became **Virgil;** the **Upper Ten, Homer;** the **Twelve, St. Catharines;** the **Lower Twenty, Jordan;** and the **Forty, Grimsby.**

The names of waterfalls are frequently associated with the pioneer mill owners who developed the water-power resource. **DeCew Falls** is close to where John DeCew established a sawmill, an oil mill for flax seed, and later a grist mill. His house gained some fame during the War of 1812 as a temporary army headquarters, the destination of Laura Secord's epic walk. When William Hamilton Merritt in 1818 borrowed a water level (a surveyor's instrument) to survey, inaccurately, the height of land between the upper waters of Twelve Mile Creek and the Welland River, DeCew accompanied him on this journey. A capstan hoist for boats on the Welland Canal was intended at this location. DeCew left the area when the first Welland Canal, constructed across the catchment area of his mill streams, curtailed the water supply, but the campus of Brock University is named after this pioneer miller.

Balls Falls provides a second example of a mill owner giving his name to the falls that begat wool and flour mills. John and George Ball were the founders. George Peter Mann Ball later proposed **Glen Elgin** as an intended town layout at this location but, bypassed by the railway, this settlement did not materialize and its milling activities declined. The area has become the **Balls Falls Conservation Area.**

Cook's Mills, named after saw and grist mills developed by the brothers Noah and Calvin Cook from Pennsylvania, was previously **Crowlandville,** the principal centre of Crowland Township. The scene of a battle during the War of 1812, Cook's Mills was considered as a location for the courthouse of Welland County.

Morse's Rapids near Smithville refers not to a miller but to Abishai Morse, a Methodist preacher who was a leader in the Temperance movement and influential in building and sustaining the Smithville High School. **The Narrows** (now **Wellandport**) is where the Big Beaver Creek nearly joins the Welland River; a narrow strip of land separating the two was cut through to provide a mill site.

Black and **Tea Creeks** in former Willoughby Township illustrate the use of colour in descriptive terminology, in this instance referring to the tint of water draining from reddish-brown swampy soils. **Tea Creek** was changed in 1973 from the incorrect "Tee Creek" at the instigation of the Willoughby Historical Museum, this request being a useful example of a local input into the official naming process. **Muddy Run,** a stream which drained to the Niagara River at the Whirlpool from **Cook's Bog,** is also named after its consistency.

Further descriptive names include **Forks Creek,** Wainfleet, where two parallel creeks united to form a fork; their union is followed by **Forks Road** to Welland. **Cave Springs,** Beamsville, combines two natural phenomena in its name. There is a **Cave of the Winds** on the American side at Niagara Falls, and **Sulphur Springs** occur in the Short Hills. In St. Catharines, Dr. Theophilus Mack developed the mineral springs by erecting the **Springbank Hotel,** where wealthy patrons might bathe in the waters that supposedly had recuperative qualities.

Swamps have been named after their characteristic vegetation: **Tamarack Swamp,** now **Willoughby Marsh; The Great Marsh** or **Cranberry Marsh,** now **Wainfleet**

A topographic feature becomes a station name associated with the Paddy Miles Express.

An incorrect spelling on the Q.E.W.. It should be Tea after the colour of the water, as at Black Creek, with both draining from Willoughby Marsh.

Marsh, and **Blackash Swamp,** Fort Erie. Marshy localities are also recalled in street names, as in **Swamp Road** which became **Niagara Stone Road.**

Marshville (now Wainfleet) arose where the Welland Feeder Canal cut through swampy land. When this land was reclaimed for agriculture, its drains were named **Eagle Marsh Drain** after bird life, and **Ellsworth** and **East Kelly Drains** after landowners. In Canborough Township **Sugar Creek Drain** signifies the maple sugar bush through which the creek flows; **James** and **Waines Drains** are named after the petitioners for drainage, as are the nearby **Mazi,**

Mitchener and **Chick-Hartnett Drains. Mill Ditch** drains into Lake Erie at Port Colborne.

Pike Creek, which flows into the Grand River near Cayuga, is after its fish life at a time when water backed into the creek before the advent of control dams. **Kraft Drain,** Fort Erie, runs through property owned by the Mennonite Kraft family, a name now closely associated with packaged cheese and other advances in food processing developed by J.L. Kraft.

2.
Indian
And French
Antecedents

Indian names provide a limited but ever-present reminder that, for thousands of years before European penetration of Niagara, aboriginal people lived on its land and made use of its water. Subsistence agriculture became established, as did semi-permanent villages, hunting camps and trails. Portages developed around the major obstacles to movement on water, such as the rapids, falls and gorge of the Niagara River. French occupancy and domination follow, notably at **Fort Niagara** on what is today the American side of the Niagara River. This garrison capitulated in 1759, and France relinquished her possessions in North America to British control in 1763.

THE INDIAN HERITAGE

The oldest recorded names are of native origin, but the memory of these names in the landscape is incomplete. In this respect considerable contrasts exist between Southern Ontario and Western Canada. The deliberate allocation of British names by the first Lieutenant Governor of Upper Canada ignored the native patterns. In any case, when the white man arrived, the sparse Indian settlements in the Peninsula had often been abandoned after destructive tribal wars. For example, the **Neutral Indians** were displaced by the **Iroquois** shortly after 1650; a burial ground at St. Davids provides only the archaeological reminder of their early presence.

However, limited traces survive in the modern landscape, and some places still carry or formerly carried a given Indian name. The **Iroquois Trail**, so called because it followed the shoreline of glacial Lake Iroquois, is now prosaically **Regional Road 81,** known locally as **St. Paul** and **Queenston Streets** in St. Catharines, **King Street** in Beamsville, and **Main Street** in Grimsby. The **Mohawk Trail** followed the crest of the Niagara Escarpment, and joined the Iroquois Trail at St. Davids to cross the Niagara River at Queenston-Lewiston. A **Lakeshore Trail** followed Lake Ontario, but shoreline erosion has eliminated most of the remnant traces.

The first vessel on the Niagara River at the falls was named **Maid of the Mist.** Launched in 1846 as a ferry for carriages and stage coaches, it soon carried sightseers. Its successors have borne the same name. Derived from a dubious Indian legend and publicized in 1851 by Andrew Burke in a tourist guide to Niagara Falls, it probably had an earlier popularity. Supposedly to appease the Thunder God Hinum and his sons who lived in the caves behind the Horseshoe Falls, a beautiful maiden was sent over the falls annually. Colourful bare-busted Victorian depictions of this sacrificial ceremony helped foster the legend. The name has been extended to the **Maid of the Mist Pool, Maid of the Mist Incline Railway** and **Maid of the Mist Landing.**

A popular vessel at the American and Horseshoe Falls takes its name from an Indian legend.

The site of a palisaded Neutral Indian village dated to 1615-1630 A.D., on the crest of the Niagara Escarpment in south St. Catharines, has become the **Barbican Heights** subdivision, barbican meaning a fortification. Indian villages may underlie the modern centres of Niagara-on-the-Lake, St. Catharines and Fort Erie, but these possibilities are not reflected in their names. Obviously much has been lost, as the French and then the British took over and developed former Indian lands. The principal surviving words of Indian terminology are **Canada, Ontario, Erie, Chippawa, Mississauga, Onondaga** and **Niagara.** Indian names introduced at a later date include **Brant, Oneida** and **Winona.**

Some Indian phonetic names with their literal descriptions of place, recorded in early accounts include Eight Mile Creek, **Ke-sick-e-con** (White cedar place); Ten Mile Creek, **Me-kis-ewan-ce** (Eagles' nest place); Twelve Mile Creek, **Es-que-sink** (Last creek in, going down lake); Fifteen and Sixteen Mile Creeks, **Nau-swan-sink** (Two creeks near together); Forty Mile Creek, **Mos-squa-waunk** (Salt lick where deer resort); Niagara Falls, **Kah-keje-wung** (The water falls); Burlington Bay, **De-o-na-sa-de-o** (Where the sand forms a bar); Queenston, **Do-che-ha-o** (Where the mountain dies in the river); and Twenty Mile Creek, **Ke-nach-daw** (Lead River).

Names of Indian origin present considerable problems of interpretation. They had to be translated from a nasal, non-written oral language to written forms by people neither trained in philology nor necessarily interested in Indian culture. The descriptive sounds must often have been passed on by word of mouth by explorers, fur traders and early settlers, who, like the Indians, had dialects and accents, and may also have been illiterate or poorly educated. Often, the French interpretations of Indian sounds had then to be rephrased in English. The resultant, derived Indian name then became stabilized and accepted long before Amerindian indigenous languages were a realm for scholarly study. There are probabilities rather than certainties when presenting the meaning of Indian names.

CANADA AND ONTARIO

Canada, now the nation-state, may be derived from "kanata", a Huronian expression meaning "a village" or "settlement". The word, first applied to the future site of Quebec City by Jacques Cartier, soon referred to the area subject to control from that village. It was then applied to a more extensive region, first north, and then south of the river and the Gulf of St. Lawrence. The provinces of **Upper Canada** and **Lower Canada** were recognized in 1791. They joined as the **Province of Canada** in 1841, and with Nova Scotia and New Brunswick became the **Dominion of Canada** in 1867. The addition of Rupert's Land and British Columbia extended **Canada** from sea to sea by 1871. The analogy of the Roman Empire has been noted for the vast expansion of area from a local name to a continental domain.

Ontario, probably a Huron name first applied to the lake, may mean a "good", "large" or "beautiful" lake, or "sparkling waters". Either interpretation could be true, though a naming after the Entouhonorons, now better known as the Seneca, has been suggested. The French called it **Lac Frontenac,** after the Governor General of New France from 1672 to 1698, and then in transition to present nomenclature, **Lac Frontenac ou Ontario.** It has also been known as **Lake of the Iroquois, Lake Saint Louis, Lake Cadavachqui, Lake Cadaracqui** and **Lake St. Lawrence.**.

The province of **Ontario,** named after the lake, came into existence in 1867. Previously the Niagara Peninsula was part of **New France,** which became **Quebec,** then **Upper Canada** after 1791 and **Canada West** after 1840.

INDIAN TRIBAL NAMES

The **Erie** or **Cat** Nation, in French **Erié (Nation du Chat),** lived south of the lake that was given this name. Earlier cartographic inscriptions include **Mer Douce, Lac Erié ou du Chat,** and **Lac Erié ou Teiocharoutiono.** The name Erié, but without its accent or accents, survives on the American side in the city of **Erie,** Pennsylvania, and in the **Erie Canal** and **Erie County,** New York. In Canada **Fort Erie** was located at the point of discharge from Lake Erie into the Niagara River. The fort gave its name to the merchant-pioneer settlement that arose in its vicinity. It has been extended to the modern town of **Fort Erie,** and **Erie Beach** is the name of a former amusement park and now a residential community.

Chippawa is the modern spelling for the village of that name at the the mouth of the Welland River (previously Chippawa Creek). The name is an Americanized version of Ojibway (Ojibwa), dropping the first syllable, then being popularized through various forms such as **Cheapway, Chippewaya, Chipweigh** and **Chippewa.** This tribal group greatly assisted the British cause during the American Revolution.

When the Niagara Portage was transferred from the east (now American) bank of the Niagara River to the Canadian west bank in the 1790s after the American Revolution, **Fort Chippawa** (also called **Fort Welland, The Block House** and **Upper Landing**) was located at its point of confluence with the Niagara River. Named after its location on Chippawa Creek, it in turn gave rise to the village of **Chippawa,** now part of the city of Niagara Falls. The **Chippawa Channel** of the Niagara River lies between the Niagara River Parkway and Grand Island. The **Chippawa Power Canal** diverts water from the Welland River to the Sir Adam Beck hydro-electric power project at Queenston.

As part of the assimilative process in British North-America, **Chippawa Creek** was by proclamation of 1792 named the **Welland River.** But the old has survived, and it is still popularly **Chippawa Creek** to this day, a pleasing survival from the past, but not a name that is recognized officially in the **Gazetteer of Canada.** Another failure to achieve a new name relates to the **Grand River,** which Simcoe attempted to call the **Ouse** after that river in Yorkshire, England, but it soon reverted to its impressive and accustomed usage.

The Mississauga Indians are recalled in **Fort Mississauga** (not Mississagua), constructed in 1814 after the burning of Niagara (now Niagara-on-the-Lake). Bricks from the town and a lighthouse on the site were used to construct the central tower and its surrounding fortifications in the form of a five-pointed star. Mississauga, from the Algonquin word meaning "large outlet", was used because the site for the fort was part of a purchase from that group of Indians, named the **Mississagas** in the Deed of Surrender, 1781.

The **Onondaga Escarpment,** locally "the ridge", is a reminder of the Onondaga tribal group who in the 15th century amalgamated with the Seneca, Cayuga, Oneida and Mohawk Indians in present New York State to form an ethnic federation known as the "Confederacy of the Five Nations" or "League of the Iroquois" from their common language. When joined by the Tuscarora Indians after 1722, this grouping became the "League of the Six Nations". **Indian Line** marks the edge of the **Six Nations Reserve,** and **Mohawk Bay** and **Mohawk Point** are associated

That's M. .i. .s. .s. .i. .s. . .

Witness the difficulties which can arise when the names of Indian Nations are translated from an oral language to written English.

Indian names on Lake **Erie.**

Streets named after **Brant** in Niagara Falls, Dunnville and Welland recall Joseph Brant, the Loyalist Mohawk war chief who was granted land on the Grand River for his people in recompense for losses suffered during the American Revolutionary War. Thayendanegea was his true Indian name, Brant being a contraction from either Barnet or Bernard, his mother's second husband after the death of his father.

Streets carrying the name **Tecumseh** in Fort Erie and St. Catharines are after this Shawnee war chief who also fought for the British against American territorial expansion. Fort Erie, remembering its Indian past, has named streets in its Oakhill Forest and Ridgewood subdivisions after **Hiawatha, Mohawk** and **Shawnee. Tecumseh, Ozark, Caribou** and **Portage** have been added for good measure.

When at Confederation the Province of Ontario supplanted Canada West, the small community of **Ontario** near Stoney Creek changed its name to **Winona.** Winona is after a Sioux word "We-non-ah" meaning the first born daughter, possibly of the Indian Chief Tecumseh and perhaps suggested by the use of this name for an American city. The name may also mean soft and beautiful, which would apply to the Chief's daughter. The prefix "Win" has given rise to the story that the place is named after the beautiful, soft wines that are produced in the vicinity.

The allusion carries forward into literature. Longfellow wrote: "Fair Nokomis bore a daughter, and she called her Wenonah." And in **The Land of Spirits,** the first contemporary native ballet to be produced in Canada (in 1988 at the National Arts Centre), an Indian legend is recalled. Earth is created when Winona, a beautiful maiden falls from heaven. Animals greet her arrival and, when the maligned Spirit of the Underworld tries to lure her into the dark Land of the Spirits, she is saved by the Creator who weds her. Few places, anywhere, have such an illustrious and euphonious name.

The **Oneida Observation Tower,** constructed in 1964, is an introduced advertising name used to promote this silverware company which moved from Oneida, New York,

Note the many and varied uses of the name Niagara, one of the best known names in North America.

to Niagara Falls, Ontario. The Oneida Indians of Iroquoian stock formed one of the Six Nations, and Oneida, New York, was named after this tribal grouping.

NIAGARA

Niagara, the most prevalent Indian name at the Frontier, has at least 39 variations in spelling on record. It is probably of Iroquoian or Neutral Indian origin. Its various documented spellings include Ongniaahra, Onguiaahra, Unghiara and Oniagara. Various interpretations exist. One authority suggests "a point of land cut in two", which superbly describes how the continuity of the Niagara Peninsula as a "land bridge" between Lake Ontario and Lake Erie is broken by the formidable gorge and rapids of the Niagara River. Another source considers the meaning to be "thunder of waters" or "resounding with great noise". A later suggestive interpretation of the Mohawk **Oh-nya-ka-ra** is that it means "on or at the neck (the Niagara River) joining the head (Lake Erie) to the body (Lake Ontario)". Although the meaning is uncertain, Niagara as a name was adopted

and applied by the French to the fort at the mouth of the Niagara River on its east (now American) bank, which is still called **Fort Niagara.**

The land haulage route on the east side of the river was developed by the Indians for countless generations before the arrival of Europeans. Used by the French and later the British as the **Niagara Portage** to bypass the tortuous middle length of the Niagara River, it has become **Portage Road** through Niagara Falls, New York.

Niagara Frontier, a common expression dating from the War of 1812, was applied primarily to the American side of the river, but sometimes included both banks. Its modern inland extent is difficult to place though, as canals bypassed the portage system, it may be deemed to encompass the area from St. Catharines to Port Colborne on the Canadian side where the Welland Canal was routed in 1829, and to Lockport, New York, where the Erie canal crossed the Niagara Escarpment in 1825. The term is now used in New York State as a sobriquet for the metropolitan area of Greater Buffalo, by public agencies such as the **Niagara Frontier Transit Authority** and the **Niagara Frontier State Park and Recreation Commission,** and

as the title of a journal formerly published by the Buffalo and Erie County Historical Society. In St. Catharines, three firms use Niagara Frontier in their company titles; curiously, there are none along the river frontage itself.

The name **Niagara** is used extensively in many geographical place names on both sides of the Frontier: at **Niagara Glen** below the falls; in the two cities of **Niagara Falls;** in **Niagara County,** New York, which faced former **Niagara Township,** Ontario; the **Niagara Peninsula** separates Lake Erie from Lake Ontario; the **Niagara Escarpment** provides most of the height difference between these two lakes; and the **Niagara River Parkway,** managed by the **Niagara Parks Commission,** follows the **Niagara River** upstream from **Niagara-on-the-Lake.**

The name has also been extended in corporate form to a series of public works and features associated with the Niagara River, including earlier bridges such as the **Niagara Suspension Bridge** or the **Niagara Cantilever Bridge** which crossed the gorge. Less well known are the **Niagara Cane,** a souvenir walking stick that could be purchased at shops in Niagara Falls; **Niagara Green,** a colour of bluish-green; **Niagara Gudgeon,** a small freshwater fish with an elongated and rounded body; **Niagara Thyme,** which grows on the calcareous rocks near the falls; the **Niagara Grape,** a cross between the Cassady and the Concord; **Niagara Spray,** a stone from below the falls sold to tourists; **Niagara Curl,** the name given to the cluster of curls formerly worn at the back of a lady's head; and the **Niagara Formula,** a trade union agreement achieved by the United Auto Workers in 1937.

Niagara as a proper name has extended its sway to areas and organizations at a distance from the river and its vicinity. Examples include **Niagara Credit Union, Niagara District Health Council, Niagara District Airport, Niagara College of Applied Arts and Technology, Regional Municipality of Niagara,** and the **Niagara, St. Catharines and Toronto Railway,** an important interurban system during the streetcar era. It is used as a general regional term, as in the **Niagara Heritage Series** of which this book is a part.

Niagara is used as a noun or adjective in colloquial phrases such as "a **Niagara** of junk mail", "a **Niagara** of tears", and "a **Niagara** of discordant sound". "Drink **Niagara** Dry" is clever advertising for a ginger ale. Examples from literature include, "The **Niagara** roar swelled and swelled from those human rapids"; "the flaming torrent... remains there today all seamed, and frothed, and rippled, a petrified **Niagara**"; and "voluble Victorians who expended their **Niagaras** of ink on the daytime view [of the falls]." The name Niagara is certainly well publicized by its extensive use and through the wide range of meanings associated with its name.

FRENCH NAMES

Few names of the French Régime from 1534 to 1763 have survived, despite the presence of their forts on the Niagara River and their extensive fur trade routes along the shores of Lake Erie and Lake Ontario. A small-scale map prepared in 1748 by Captain Pouchot, commandant at Fort Niagara, named the Niagara River, its portage and the **Chenonda** (now Welland) River. The Niagara Escarpment as a source of limestone was described as the **Côtes** or **Platon. Le Grand Marais** (Wainfleet Marsh) was named in the Port Colborne area. **Marais Normand, Marais à la Biche** and **Marais des Deux Sorties** (the two entrances of Fifteen and Sixteen Mile Creeks) were names applied to features along the shoreline of Lake Ontario. "Marais" is the French for marsh, and "Côte" is a hill.

English translations of French names may include **Grand Island,** from Hennepin's "La Grande Ile" of 1679. **Grand River** may be the English translation of the French "La Grande Rivière", reflecting both the size of the river at its mouth and its length.

Point Abino, named after a French Jesuit priest, Père Claude Aveneau who lived there about 1690, found its spelling changed from "v" to "b" **(Abeneau).** It ultimately emerged as **Abino** (not Albino), which retained the original sound but not the spelling. The age of the name may be indicated by the fact that "point" precedes it; elsewhere the name is placed before the headland feature it describes, as at **Windmill Point. Abino Bay** and **Abino Hills** are derived from the original names.

Frenchman's Creek may be so named as a camping place used by French voyageurs before tackling the rapids upriver at the entrance to the Niagara River. One account relates how a French group was ambushed here; as they took to their boats which overturned in mid-stream, their plumed hats floating downstream were washed ashore in the creek. Streets, buildings and social activities named after **Champlain, Frontenac, Hennepin** and **La Salle** also provide some reminder for early French explorations of the continental interior. Though the significance of the name is unknown, the **Tête-de-Pont** battery (meaning a bridgehead on the enemy side of a river south of the Welland River at Chippawa was part of the defensive system during the War of 1812.

3.
The
Pioneer Period:
A British Framework

The war fought from 1775 to 1783 between Great Britain and thirteen of her colonies in North America, variously refferred to as the "American Revolution", the "Revolutionary War", the "War of Independence" and the "War of American Independence", is critical for the settlement and the ensuing naming process at Niagara. The **United States of America** was recognized as a distinct nation at the Treaty of Paris in 1783, and the boundary between the new nation and the British colony of Quebec was then place along the Niagara River. An immediate outcome, the influx of **Loyalist** refugees to the freedom and security of British territory, involved the Niagara Peninsula intimately.

The surge of immigrant pioneer settlers required an administrative structure which included naming the districts, ridings, counties and townships that were created. With the survey fabric of townships providing the framework, pioneer settlers were granted land in numbered lots within a particular township. It became a regularized, named and numbered landscape from the largest to the smallest unit of land occupancy. Names, at first applied from above by governmental decree and compatible with the traditional organized structure of colonial administration, later emerged from local usage through individual possession, clearing and farming activities on the land.

DISTRICTS, RIDINGS AND COUNTIES

The Niagara Peninsula, a component of the old Province of Quebec, became part of the **District of Nassau** in 1788. As the other administrative districts to become Upper Canada in 1791 were **Luneburg** (later **Lunenburg**), **Mecklenburg** and **Hesse,** these Hanoverian names probably honoured the British royal family. An ancestor of George III was Countess of Nassau. Nassau was renamed the **Home District** in 1792, possibly not after a person but in the sense of either the home base or the headquarters where parliament met.

In 1798 the Home District was divided into counties, ridings and townships. The unit known as the **Niagara District** had four ridings, which together formed the **County of Lincoln** (Table 3.1). The name **Riding** a British introduction having its origins in an Old Norse word for a third, was used for the administrative division of Yorkshire, England, into North, East and South Ridings. In Canada it now means a political division or constituency that returns a Member of Parliament. Each Riding is divided into **Polling Districts** where voters cast their ballots.

As settlement expanded, new administrative units were created. In 1816 the **Gore District** was founded out of the western parts of the Niagara District, on land then known

Table 3.1
Administrative Names In The Niagara Region

Area Names

1798	1846	1965	1978
Upper Canada	Canada West	Ontario	Ontario
Home District	Niagara District	Niagara Region	Regional Municipality
Niagara District	{ County of Lincoln	County of Lincoln	of Niagara
County of Lincoln*	{ County of Welland	County of Welland	

Local Names

1798	1846 Townships	1846 Emerging Settlements	1965	1978
First Riding	**Townships**	**Emerging Settlements**	**Cities**	**Cities**
			Niagara Falls	
Caistor (ts)			St. Catharines	Niagara Falls
Clinton (ts)	Bertie --------------	Fort Erie (v)	Welland	Port Colborne
Grimsby (ts)		Waterloo (v)		St. Catharines
	Caistor		**Towns**	Thorold
Second Riding	Clinton -----------	Beamsville (v)	Beamsville	Welland
	Crowland ---------	Merrittsville (v)	Fort Erie	
Grantham (ts)		Helmsport (v)	Grimsby	**Towns**
Louth (ts)	Gainsborough		Niagara	
Niagara (ts)	Grantham ---------	Port Dalhousie (v)	Port Colborne	Fort Erie
Niagara (t)		St. Catharines (t)	Thorold	Grimsby
	Grimsby ----------	Grimsby (v)		Lincoln
Third Riding		Smithville (v)	**Villages**	Niagara-on-the-Lake
	Humberstone -----	Port Colborne (v)	Chippawa	Pelham
Pelham (ts)		Stonebridge (v)	Crystal Beach	
Stamford (ts)	Louth --------------	Jordan (v)	Fonthill	**Townships**
Thorold (ts)	Niagara -----------	Niagara (t)		
		Queenston (v)	**Townships**	Wainfleet
Fourth Riding		St. Davids (v)	Bertie	West Lincoln
	Pelham		Caistor	
Bertie (ts)	Stamford ----------	Chippawa (v)	Clinton	
Crowland (ts)		Drummondville (v)	Crowland	**Sources:**
Humberstone (ts)	Thorold ----------	Allanburg (v)	Gainsborough	
Wainfleet (ts)		Port Robinson (v)	Grimsby, North	1798 An Act for the better division of the province
Willoughby (ts)		St. Johns (v)	Grimsby, South	1846 Smith's **Canadian Gazetteer**
		Thorold (v)	Humberstone	1965 Niagara Region Local Government Review
ts = townships	Wainfleet ----------	Marshville (v)	Louth	1978 Regional Municipality of Niagara
t = towns	Willoughby		Niagara	
* = a larger territory			Pelham	
than the current			Thorold	
Niagara Region		t = town	Wainfleet	
		v = village	Willoughby	

Table 3.1

generally as the **Head-of-the-Lake** because of its location at the western extremity of Lake Ontario. The Act specified that the district town was to be located on land owned by George Hamilton, son of Robert Hamilton, the Queenston merchant whose wife is recalled in the name **St. Catharines.** The act also indicated that the town was to bear the name **Hamilton.**

The Gore District eventually comprised Halton and Wentworth Counties, and parts of Wellington and Brant Counties. The former provides a neat juxtaposition of associated names. Frances **Gore** was the third Lieutenant Governor of Upper Canada, his wife was Annabella **Went-**

worth Gore, and William **Halton** was the Governor's secretary. Wellington refers to the Duke of Wellington, and Brant to Joseph **Brant,** the Mohawk Indian Chief with a land grant at the head of Burlington Bay.

The counties of Lincoln and Haldimand remained, and together comprised the Niagara District. In 1840 the four ridings of Lincoln County were regrouped into two ridings, the **North Riding** being the unification of the First and Second Ridings, and the **South Riding** the former Third and Fourth Ridings. Five years later, North Riding became the **County of Lincoln** and South Riding the **County of Welland.**

When the Niagara District was abolished in 1850, it included the Counties of Haldimand, Lincoln and Welland. Haldimand became independent in 1850, and Welland in 1856. Lincoln remained, but much smaller in area. Lincoln and Welland Counties survived until 1970, when they were dissolved and amalgamated with their municipalities to form the present **Regional Municipality of Niagara,** known locally as **The Region** or **Regional Niagara.** (Table 3.1).

The name for **Lincoln County** originated with Colonel John Graves Simcoe, the first Lieutenant Governor of Upper Canada, who arrived at Niagara in 1792. He wanted British government, the established church, hereditary titles and the place names of England. As an integral part of this strategy to counterbalance the new American Republic, a series of British names was introduced. **Lincoln** was derived from Lincolnshire, England. **Welland** is after the Welland River, in turn from the River Welland in the same English county. **Haldimand** commemorates Sir Frederick Haldimand, first Governor of the British province of Quebec, 1763-1791, responsible for settling Loyalist refugees in the Niagara Peninsula and Upper Canada.

The now forgotten **Monck County,** an electoral division created in 1867 to balance constituencies in Ontario with those in Quebec, included townships from Haldimand, Lincoln and Welland Counties. Sir Charles Stanley Monck was Governor General of Canada from 1861 to 1867. The constituency returned members to parliament until Haldimand was re-established in 1903.

THE TOWNSHIP NAMES

The administrative process of the 1780s to settle the land required the division of the Home District into territorial divisions known as **Townships. Niagara Township** in the northeast quadrant of the Niagara Peninsula, the first area to be settled, was **Township No.1. Township No. 2,** briefly called Mount Dorchester after the Governor General, Lord Dorchester, became **Stamford Township.** Townships were then numbered west along the shore of Lake Ontario, **Township No. 3** becoming Grantham Township (now St. Catharines), and **Township No.4** Louth Township.

These numbered townships were named by Lieutenant Governor Simcoe in accordance with his policy of replicating Britain in Upper Canada. Further, Simcoe did not respect Indian names; thus **Toronto** was renamed **York** in honour of Prince Edward, Duke or York, and its previous Indian name was not restored until 1834.

At Niagara, Simcoe used names mostly from Lincolnshire, England (Fig. 3.2). Its villages and towns supplied the township names of **Caistor, Crowland, Gainsborough, Grantham, Grimsby Humberstone** (from Humberston), **Louth, Stamford, Wainfleet,** and **Willoughby.** Each has an earlier meaning, steeped in the history of the British Isles; for example, the two "by" suffixes of Danish origin mean the village or homestead of Grim in **Grimsby,** and the village among willows in **Willoughby. Caistor** refers to a Roman fort, **Gainsborough** is Gejn's burg and **Grantham** is Granta's village.

It is fanciful exercise to relate the meaning of the English name to the circumstances of landscape at Niagara. Nor should the character of the place that has emerged at Niagara be compared with its English equivalent; the cultural transfusion of a name provides the only genuine link between the two places.

NIAGARA'S TOWNSHIPS: A CULTURAL TRANSFER FROM LINCOLNSHIRE, ENGLAND

Fig. 3.2

Other Niagara names with direct Lincolnshire associations include **Thorold,** after Sir John Thorold, an M.P. for Lincolnshire interested in colonial policy. **Clinton** is probably a family name; Lord Clinton was created Earl of Lincoln in 1472 and Sir Henry Clinton was in command of the British forces in America from 1778 to 1782. There is a village of Pilham in Lincolnshire, but **Pelham** was probably named after Charles A. Pelham, M.P. in 1792 for Lincolnshire, England, and a personal friend of Simcoe. Pelham was the family name of the Duke of Newcastle; several members held office in the reigns of George II and III. **Bertie** (now Fort Erie) was named after Sir Peregrine Bertie, third Duke of Ancaster, 19th Baron Willoughby, who supported the Canada Bill in the House of Lords. Though a Lincolnshire place name has been noted previously for Willoughby, it is also possible that he is reflected in the naming of Willoughby and Bertie as adjacent townships.

An earlier association with Niagara is evident in names further afield. **Ancaster, Barton, Binbrook** and **Saltfleet** have the same direct associations with Lincolnshire, England, as do many of the township names in Lincoln and Welland Counties. They were formerly part of the Niagara District and subject to the same naming process.

NEW CENTRES IN THE TOWNSHIPS

Retaining the now established and traditional name, the survey townships became the units of administration for the purposes of local government when **Municipal Corporations** were established in 1850. The Townships of **Caistor, Clinton, Gainsborough, Grantham, Grimsby, Louth** and **Niagara** were incorporated in the County of Lincoln, and at the same date the townships of **Bertie, Crowland, Humberstone, Pelham, Stamford, Thorold, Wainfleet** and **Willoughby** were incorporated in the County of Welland.

New settlements were introduced to the Niagara Peninsula within its collage of townships. These centres arose and progressed from one status to another, as population and the need for services expanded (Fig. 3.3). An example from Grantham Township is **Merritton;** incorporated as a Village in 1874, it became a Town in 1918 and amalgamated

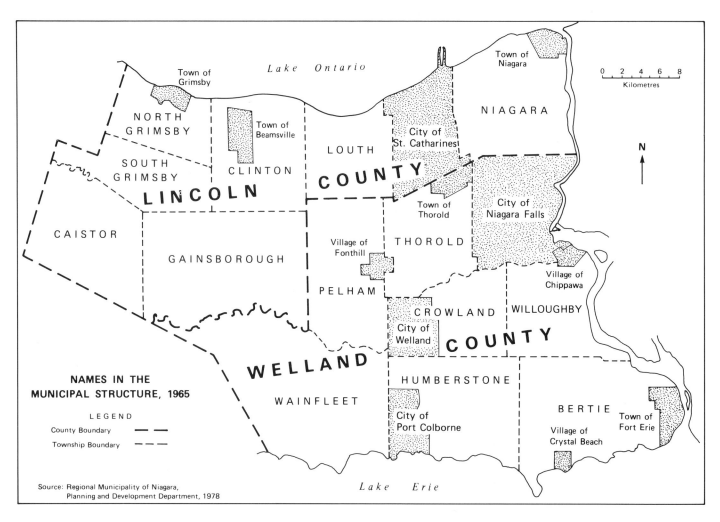

Fig. 3.3

with St. Catharines in 1961. **Grimsby** incorporated as a Village in 1876, became a Town in 1878 and a City in 1917.

"Police Villages", an early form of local government to organize police services in small communities, were also established; "erected" being the official terminology. They include **Campden,** 1905; **Queenston** and **Smithville,** 1911; **Jordan Station,** 1915; **Fenwick,** 1919 and **St. Davids,** 1923; and **Vineland,** 1925.

Administrative change in association with the naming process can be very complicated. **Elgin,** incorporated as the **Town of Clifton** in 1856, changed its name to **Niagara Falls** in 1881. It then amalgamated with the **Village of Niagara Falls** (previously **Drummondville**), and was incorporated as the **City of Niagara Falls** in 1903.

32

Thorold coat of arms

A second example of this involved process is provided by **Fort Erie.** Incorporated as a Village in 1857, it was annexed to the **Town of Bridgeburg** and incorporated as the **Town of Fort Erie** in 1931. Previously **International Bridge,** incorporated as a Village in 1894, had amalgamated with the **Village of Amigari** as the **Village of Bridgeburg** in 1895. Incorporated as a Town in 1915, the name was changed to **Fort Erie** in 1931.

THE SURVIVAL OF COUNTY AND TOWNSHIP NAMES

Even though now dissolved, the county names of Lincoln and Welland remain well entrenched in the modern landscape. They have survived as relic memories in active use by private, business and government agencies. Prime examples include the **Lincoln County Board of Education** the **Lincoln County Roman Catholic Separate School Board** and the **Welland County Separate School Board.**

Lincoln County is used in corporate names such as the

Lincoln County Academy of Medicine Secretarial Service, Lincoln County Cancer Society, Lincoln County Law Association Library** and the **Lincoln County Women Teachers Association.** Lincoln is incorporated in the name of at least twenty private businesses in the former county seat of St. Catharines. The present **Town of Lincoln** revives an old name, but it occupies only a small portion of the former county and is of lower administrative status. **Beamsville,** perhaps a more suitable name for this town, would have been in accord with the extensive areas allotted to places like Fort Erie or Port Colborne when local government was reformed at 1970, but we are also grateful that the Lincoln name has been perpetuated.

The now defunct Welland County is recalled in the **Welland County General Hospital, Welland County Law Library** and **Welland County Motorcycle Club,** each in Welland. Armouries in St. Catharines and Niagara Falls still house the **Lincoln and Welland Regiment** with its direct lineage to Butler's Rangers and known popularly as the **Lincs and Winks.** Past and important traditions die hard.

Of the original townships, the names **Grimsby, Pelham, Thorold** and **Wainfleet** have survived, and are well used in their respective communities by business and social groups. The now obsolete township names also remain entrenched. Grantham, taken over by St. Catharines, is well recalled in this city by activities that include **Grantham Bakery, Grantham Fitness Centre, Grantham Home Hardware, Grantham Lions Club, Grantham Mennonite Brethren Church, Grantham Optimist Youth Centre, Grantham Shopping Plaza** and **Grantham United Church.** Of particular interest is that Howard Engel has used **Grantham** as a "fictitious" name for St. Catharines in the 1980s. A noted local writer of mystery stories, his landmarks are thinly disguised, and the city is recognizable.

Crowland is recalled in Welland by the name still visible on its former civic hall, as well as by the **Crowland Hotel,** the **Crowland Sports Club** and two businesses. **Bertie** is remembered in the town of Fort Erie by the **Bertie Boating Club,** the **Bertie Brethren in Christ Church** and by local businesses. Reminders of **Willoughby** are **Willoughby Historical Museum, Willoughby Manor, Willoughby Marsh** and the **Willoughby Volunteer Fire Department.** West Lincoln has the **Caistor Community Centre,** and **Humberstone** survives in businesses at Port Colborne including the **Humberstone International Speedway** as a sporting activity. **Louth** is recalled frequently by names in both St. Catharines and Lincoln.

To the west of Regional Niagara, when the Regional Municipality of Hamilton-Wentworth came into existence in 1974, **Stoney Creek** and **Saltfleet** were merged. Saltfleet had most of the population, land area and assessment, but **Stoney Creek** survived as the name for the larger unit, perhaps because it was better known, having been the site of a battle between British and American forces during the War of 1812. To the south, **Glanford** and **Binbrook** were amalgamated as **Glanbrook,** using one syllable from each name. "Binglan" "Glanbin" and "Binford" were presumably not acceptable because of their unharmonious sounds.

NAMES AFTER DISTINGUISHED PERSONS

After American Independence, roads, settlements and their defensive systems had necessarily to be relocated on the British (now Canadian) side of the Niagara River. The **Niagara Portage** or **Carrying Place** to the Upper Great Lakes on the now American side lost its traffic, became the **Old Portage,** and is now **Portage Road** in Niagara Falls, New York.

To bypass the tortuous middle length of the Niagara River, a **New Portage** was constructed on the Canadian side between Queenston and Chippawa. Known also as the **Road Through the Settlements,** it began on private land, became a lawful road in 1802, and before the Welland Canal was the most important route for transportation. Though now broken in the north by the hydro reservoir at Queenston Heights and named **Main Street** where it crosses Lundy's Lane, this route survives almost intact through Niagara Falls as **Portage Road.** It should be signed and glorified as the first **King's Highway** in Upper Canada. The term King's Highway is still in use by the provincial government for its principal routes, despite the long reign of Queen Elizabeth II. **Stamford Green,** the rare feature of New England village green in Canada, is situated on the Portage Road.

Queenston, known as **(The) New Landing, (The) Landing,** and **(The) West Landing** to distinguish it from the American side, was also **The Lower Settlement** to distinguish it from **The Upper Settlement** (Chippawa). It became **Queen's Town,** which either honours Queen Charlotte or was chosen because Lieutenant Governor Simcoe had commanded the Queen's Rangers from 1776 to 1781 during most of the war period. Elided to **Queenstown,** it became shortened to **Queenston.**

Fort George, Niagara-on-the-Lake, is named after King George III of England who reigned from 1751 to 1820, the period during which the new United States of America separated from British North America. Constructed to command the Niagara passage to inland North America, it was built in 1797 and became the most important British fort at the Niagara Frontier. Captured by American troops but then regained by the British during the War of 1812, it was abandoned in the 1820s. Restored as a make-work project during the Depression of the late 1930s, Fort George is now a major tourist attraction.

Queenston Heights, named after the relief feature it commands, was the site for the battle of that name fought against invading American troops in October 1812. A stone gateway, steps and a path of Renaissance formality focus on the imposing landmark of **Brock's Monument.** The monument commemorates **Sir Isaac Brock,** the general who commanded the victorious British troops, but who also lost his life at the Battle of Queenston Heights. Nearby are the earlier fortifications of **Forts Drummond** and **Riall,** named in honour of these British generals. About half a kilometre to the west is **Sheaffe's Pass** (or **Path**), where General Sheaffe ascended "the mountain".

Brock, through fame at Queenston Heights and with previous successes in repulsing the American invasions, is known as "The Saviour of Upper Canada". **St. Saviours Anglican Church,** Queenston, recalls this patriotic appellation.

If Brock was the "hero" of the War of 1812, then Laura Ingersoll Secord was its "heroine". She walked from Queenston to DeCew Falls to warn British forces of an impending American attack, is buried in Drummmond Hill Cemetery, Niagara Falls, and commemorated by a monument at Queenston Heights. Her farm house at Queenston has been restored as a visitor attraction. **Secord** is a not uncommon name in the Peninsula, as illustrated by **Secord Road** and **Secord Woods**, a subdivision in St. Catharines.

The Niagara Escarpment and Stamford Township were both at first named **Mount Dorchester** to commemorate Lord Dorchester, the Governor of Quebec in 1768. This imperial name survives in **Dorchester Street**, Niagara-on-the-Lake; and in the **Dorchester Manor** retirement home

in Niagara Falls. A further association with Lord Dorchester exists in the Short Hills where **Becketttown** or **Becketts Mills**, named after Samuel Beckett from Pennsylvania who obtained a post office 1867, was renamed **Effingham** to honour the wife of the Governor General. Lord Dorchester married Lady Maria, daughter of the second Earl of Effingham, in 1772.

FROM NEWARK TO NIAGARA-ON-THE-LAKE

The place that functioned as the first capital of Upper Canada, the major town of the Niagara District and the county seat for the extensive county of Lincoln, has been known by a series of names. The settlement was at first called **Loyalist Village** after its inhabitants, **West Niagara** as an offshoot across the river from Fort Niagara, and **Butlersbury** after Colonel John Butler who raised and commanded the **Butler's Rangers** out of Fort Niagara during the American Revolution; Butlersbury near Johnstown, New York, was his former home. Many of the officers and men who served in Butler's Rangers settled in the Niagara Peninsula. Butler then served as a judge and as deputy superintendent of Indian Affairs and was a key member of the local pioneer society. **Butlersbury** seems to have been changed, by mistake or because of more common usage, to **Butlersburg.**

The town was surveyed as **Lenox** (not Lennox) in 1791, presumably after Charles, third Duke of Richmond and Lennox, Master General of the Ordnance in London at the time. Renamed **Newark** by Simcoe in 1792, one reference suggests this word could refer to that place in New Jersey, the previous home of many settlers. Another suggestion is "New Ark", a refuge where the immigrant Loyalists could rebuild their shattered lives in new surroundings. It could also mean "'New Work", meaning the creation of a new centre. Not impossible is that Newark could be derived from Newark-on-Trent, Nottinghamshire, England; the analogy of its castle supporting the Royalist cause and resisting three sieges during the Civil War might have appealed to Simcoe.

After Simcoe's departure, **Newark** reverted in 1798 to **Niagara** by popular sentiment. Like the imposed names for the Chippawa and Ouse rivers, these English names were neither indigenous nor part of tradition, but placed on the landscape to stress its links. The first immigrants, United Empire Loyalists, were British in spirit and allegiance, but they had lived in the colonies for several decades, and the majority had been born outside the British Isles.

Niagara persisted as the official name throughout the nineteenth century. Meantime, **Niagara Falls** to the south was founded, and took over the Niagara name. To avoid confusion with its urban neighbour, the post office at Niagara was renamed **Niagara-on-the-Lake** in 1902, but the traditional name **Niagara** remained for both the township and the town. The "Borough of Niagara-on-the-Lake" was proposed in 1965 when amalgamation of the two units was suggested in a review of local government, and this historically inaccurate name was awarded in 1970 when the **Town of Niagara-on-the-Lake** was created. Though Niagara-on-the-Lake is a pleasing name for a town of great architectural and historic character with the distinction of having a Lord Mayor, the long established tradition of a well-known and accustomed name had been lost. **Niagara** as the "true" name does however survive unofficially in habitual use by local residents.

AMERICAN EXPRESSSIONS

Not surprisingly, because of their location next to the United States and because many immigrants were from that country, the new British settlements at Niagara acquired several American forms of speech. "Township", in its English form, means a small town or village as part of a large parish, certainly not the situation at Niagara where the township boundaries were drawn through forest and the settler had to clear this land of its cover to permit agriculture. Urbanity and settled circumstances did not exist.

Township was used in the American sense of the formalized and regular-sized tracts into which public lands acquired from the Indians were divided before their sale. This land survey unit, awarded certain powers of government as a division of the county, provided the foundation of municipal organization. The transition from "townships" in the forest to their modern urban countenance has involved decades of change and achievement.

A second American introduction is "Creek", which in its English sense means a part of the sea that penetrates into the land. Its Canadian meaning as the tributary of a larger river (Lyons Creek as a tributary of the Welland River), or as a freshwater stream smaller than a river (the creeks that flow into Lake Ontario), is American usage. However, softening the word from its English pronunciation of Krek to krik seems not to have occurred.

"Brook", the English equivalent, is hardly used at Niagara; **Binbrook,** an exception, is a name introduced from England by Simcoe. Nor is "stream" used for a small watercourse, though the word is common in the Atlantic Provinces.

Another Americanism is to capitalize "River", and to place it after the descriptive proper name. In England it is the river or River Welland; at Niagara, it is the Welland River.

"Pond" would seem to be used in the American sense of obstructing a stream so that it forms a pond. "Lake" would be the equivalent English word for the "ponds" along Lake Ontario; in England a "pond" is small and of artificial creation, like a duck-, fish- or mill-pond.

The emphasis on "Point", as a promontory of land projecting into water as at **Shisler Point** or **Windmill Point** may also be American usage. The more likely English word is "headland" or "head", for example **Beachy Head**, though "points" do exist as at the northern end of the Isle of Man. Other American expressions, for later discussion, include "Corners" and "Main Street".

4.
Naming
The Pioneer
Landscape

The districts and townships were named by official decree, but the early settlers identified their surroundings by names that were familiar to them. Not only villages, towns, creeks and roads were so named, but also mills, farms and fields in a possessive manner after a person or a family associated with that feature. Many of these individual names have been lost or changed through time. Many others have survived and been formalized, to express the qualities of local pride and traditional association with the landscape. Landscape was provided with a personal meaning that can be traced through local histories. Social serendipity (the faculty of making fortunate and unexpected discoveries by accident) is certainly a factor when sudying the thousands of personal names that exist.

A PERSONALIZED LANDSCAPE

When **Butler's Rangers** were disbanded immediately after the American Revolution, they settled with refugee families on land along the Niagara River and the Ontario lakeshore. These **Loyalist** settlers, mostly from the Mohawk Valley of New York State, were disaffected American colonists. In 1789 it was proclaimed that Loyalists and their children might add **U.E.** to their names, U.E. being initials for the "Unity of Empire" and hence the title of **United Empire Loyalists.**

The Loyalists had various backgrounds, and many were not of British origin. Some had come to the New World in the 1600s as Dutch immigrants; others arrived with the Palatine emigration of the early 1700s. They were of French, Dutch and German ancestry, although some had anglicized names. They had names such as Ball (Bahl), Bouck, Bowman (Baumann), Bradt, De Cew (De Cou), Dittrick (Dietrich), House (Haus), Keefer (Kuefer, Kieffer), Kraft (Krafft), Misener (Muisener), Secord (Sicard), Servos, Swayze, Ten Broeck, Van Every, Vrooman and Warner (Wanner), as well as British names such as Clark, Clement, Cook, Durham, Field, McMicking, McNab, Merritt, Stewart and Woodruff.

Though most were of the Protestant faith, their religion also varied. There were collectively more Lutherans, Mennonites, Methodists, Presbyterians, Quakers and Tunkers than Church of England. Their church buildings were often shared for religious services, and some settlers had to embrace another faith because a minister or priest of their own was not available. Intermarriage and a common concern with the shared features of pioneer life soon reduced the differences that existed.

The frequent use of Corners in conjunction with a pioneer name is American not British in its associations.

These immigrants add their personal names to the landscape in a variety of different ways and associations with a place. They gave their names to waterfalls (Ball's **Falls**), some became consecrated (**St.** Davids),and others have harbours (**Port** Davidson), bridges (O'Reillys **Bridge**), road junctions (Chambers **Corners**), creeks (Lyons **Creek**) or headlands (Shisler **Point**) named after them. This personalization of landscape soon became accepted through local usage; for example, **Lundy's Lane** left "Abraham Lampman's on the left, John Garner's on the right, John Silverthorn's house on the left... thence to William Lundy's on the right and Green's on the left."

The Post Office provided certain names with statutory authority as the postal system advanced with the expansion of settlement. As every place had to be given an acceptable but distinct name, postmasters had often to select between several divergent names for a given place, or provide that place with a new name. Post office names with their dates of foundation include **Niagara**, 1789; **Chippawa** and **Queenston**, 1801; **St. Catherines**, 1817; **Homer**, 1859; and **Virgil**, 1862 (note the spelling of Chippawa and St. Catherines).

"Corners", mostly with a preceding personal name and as the place where two roads meet, is rare in England but frequent at Niagara, for example, **Turners, Chambers, Pelham, Caistor** and **Black Horse Corners. Ten Broeck's Corners** were at the junction of Glendale and Merritt Streets in St. Catharines. Corners, located initially in rural areas, were local meeting places, closely related to the gridiron road network with its numerous crossover junctions. "Cross" or "Crossroads" would be the more likely English terminology.

With these kinds of place names, there appears to have been little attempt to duplicate names familiar to the immigrants from earlier home localities. The names have arisen and been applied locally through occupance of the land. In contrast Daniel Servos nostalgically named his house at Four Mile Pond **Palatine Hill**, either after the German Palatinate settlement in the Mohawk Valley, New York, or after the Palatinate in Germany, for his family came from the Rhine.

Virgil name unlikely to grace water tower

Virgil will not be immortalized on the new water tower on Highway 55 if Niagara-on-the-Lake councillors have their way.

Responding to a letter from Niagara Region's public works department, the town's administration committee decided yesterday that "Virgil" should not be painted on the tower, located in the industrial park.

"If ever we're going to have this town be the town of Niagara-on-the-Lake as opposed to individual areas and hamlets within Niagara-on-the-Lake, if anything is to go on the tower it should be Niagara-on-the-

Lake," said Ald. Lorraine Warner.

The idea of painting the tower came from the Virgil Businessmen's Association, which made a request of the Region.

The Region does not allow painting on the actual water tank but would consider permitting it on the concrete column, director of engineering Con Eidt said in his letter.

He added that his staff is willing to discuss such a proposal with the association but would require the town's approval before granting permission.

Rittenhouse, a well-known name in the Vineland area.

Let the reader decide. Is the story about the origin of Stevensville fact or fiction?

NAMES AFTER EARLY SETTLERS

Jacob Beam, who moved to the Niagara area in 1788 from New Jersey, is recognized in **Beamsville**, previously **The Harbour. Smithville**, the avowed **Hub of the Peninsula**, may reflect Smith Griffin, a Welshman who migrated to Canada via New York State and established a sawmill on the upper waters of Twenty Mile Creek. An alternative story is that **Griffinville** or **Griffintown** after Richard Griffin, a Loyalist settler, was renamed **Smithville** by his son, Smith Griffin, in memory of Mary Smith, his mother's maiden name. **Griffin Street** is the main street of Smithville.

Stevensville may have been named by the carpenter employed to build the McCarthy hotel. When the frame was erected, Mr. Stevens supposedly went to the peak and, with a bottle of liquor in hand, pronounced the name to be Stevensville. The veracity of such stories cannot be checked. Why the carpenter's name, rather than McCarthy the hotel owner's, is unexplained. Such details are folklore. They provide an interesting account, but they may or may not be correct.

Rittenhouse Road, Vineland, honours this early pioneer family, its most notable member being Moses F. Rittenhouse, a native of that village who moved to Chicago where he attained financial success in the lumber business. As a philanthropist in the spirit of his Mennonite faith, he endowed many local features, including the farm on which the Vineland Experimental Station began its operations, a community hall, a school, the village hall, road improvement, the provision of cement sidewalks, and improvements to the church and its cemetery.

Zimmerman Avenue, Niagara Falls, recalls Samuel Zimmerman, a German from Huntington County, Pennsylvania. Mostly through his efforts, the **Great Western Railway** (now **Canadian National**) was extended to the Suspension Bridge across the Niagara River, and the village of Elgin (later Niagara Falls) became a significant railway town. Zimmerman was a contractor for locks on the Second Welland Canal and for the **Great Western** and the **Erie and Ontario** railways. He founded the **Zimmerman Bank** in Niagara Falls, a building which also contained the Customs House and Post Office. His substantial estate, designed with extensive landscaped gardens in the British style, overlooked the falls to the southwest of present day Clifton Hill (then Ferry Street). He was killed in a railway accident in 1857 when his train plunged into the Desjardins Canal at Hamilton.

Pioneer names in St. Catharines include **Hainer** and **Dittrick Streets.** Their land grants faced each other across Twelve Mile Creek as did their former homes. John Hainer and Jacob Dittrick were the first settlers at this meeting point of streams. Both subscribed to obtain the first church, now St. George's Anglican Church. William **Facer,** a pioneer Grantham farmer, is recalled in **Facer Street.** **Adams Street** is after Thomas Adams, who owned the sawmill on Twelve Mile Creek that was purchased by William Hamilton Merritt. This site is of great historical importance. Situated at the southern end of modern **Welland Vale Island**, its source of water gradually diminished as settlement expanded. This catastrophe in turn encouraged its owner to seek an alternative water supply, which became the initiating action that introduced the Welland Canal to the Niagara Peninsula.

Lundy's Lane, Niagara Falls, is after William Lundy, who lived on its south side. An Indian trail before the township survey, the land was given from the grant owned by Charles Green and declared a public road at the same time as the Beaver Dams Road. Why then not **Green Lane** rather than Lundy's Lane? Lundy could have been more of a leader among settlers but, as one account of 1887 has stated, "the people who first named the road made use of 'apt alliterations artful aid'... . The words beginning with two L's are more euphonious than would be a name the initials of which are G.L."

This explanation could be witticism but, whatever the truth, Lundy's Lane became etched into the Canadian vocabulary of place names when a bloody British-American battle was fought in its vicinity in July 1814. The retention of "Lane", a narrow way between fences or hedges, is an interesting anachronism for a modern, four-lane highway lined by commercial and tourist developments.

Changing circumstances sometimes resulted in name changes as well. **Street's Creek** was named after Samuel Street but became **Usshers Creek** after John Ussher married Street's only daughter. John Burch (Birch) gave his name to saw and grist mills constructed in 1786 near the present site of the Toronto Power Generating Station at Niagara Falls; **Burch's Mills**, the first to use the power of the Niagara River near the falls, were purchased after his death in 1797 by Samuel Street, and became **Street's Mills.** Upstream, **Canby's Mills** named after Benjamin Canby, were the site of an early tourist attraction, the **Burning Spring**, where natural gas bubbling through the water was fed into a pipe and lighted. Canby moved to **Canby Town**, later **Canby's Borough** which became **Canborough**, a name often shortened to **Canboro'** or the slang of **Canboro.**

Fonthill (not Font Hill), formerly **Osborne's Corners** after the settler James Osborne, then **Temperanceville**, was perhaps named after a spring that fed a drinking fountain on the Canboro Road; a designation after Fonthill Abbey, England, has also been suggested. Nearby **Steeles Corners** has changed from a personal appellation to **Ridgeville**, a reference to its physical setting.

St. Johns, not St. Johns West, is possibly after John Street and John Darling, two early settlers, and was known as **Streets Mills** after the former individual. **Stumptown**, describing the pioneer landscape where tree stumps left in the ground characterized clearing for several years, became **St. George** after George Keefer, then **Thorold** as the major centre in the township of that name. **St. Davids**, previously **Four Mile Mills** and **Davidsville**, is after Major David Secord of Butler's Rangers who settled in the area.

Gentlemen's estates add their patina of splendour to the landscape, as wealthy early settlers built imposing houses.

An Italian name has been given to the principal park in downtown St. Catharines.

To show their prestige, the residences were often named in some distinct way. Some expressed the natural circumstances of the surrounding landscape: **The Wilderness, Willowbank, Oakhill** and **Maplehurst.** Other owners drew attention to the importance of their residence by adding **Hall,** to denote its status as a real or supposed mansion on a landed estate. An early example is **Rodman Hall** after a family name. Later, Sir Harry Oakes named his home **Oak Hall.**

"Cottage", "Croft" and "Lodge", in reverse modesty for spacious homes, were also used; for instance **Lake Lodge** as the country home of Rev. Robert Addison of Niagara-on-the-Lake; **Suncroft** as the mansion on Church Street, St. Catharines, owned by James McSloy; **Foxcroft,** St. Catharines, as the residence of Harold Fox, a distinguished patent lawyer; and **Roslyn Cottage,** on Queen Street, Niagara-on-the-Lake, built circa 1832 by Ralph Morden Crysler, a wealthy merchant.

Landed gentry also had stately homes: Sir Peregrine Maitland purchased **Stamford Park** on the brow of the Niagara Escarpment south of St. Davids in 1822; **Mount Dorchester,** not to be confused with the early name for the

Niagara Escarpment, was the nearby home of Justice William Dummer Powell when Niagara was the capital; and **Clark Hill,** an estate on high ground northwest of Dufferin Islands, was the home of Colonel Clark who commanded the Second Lincoln Militia during the War of 1812. A later name is **Montebello** from Italy as the intended name for a house to be built by a son of W.H. Merritt, but he died before its completion; it became **Montebello Park** when the land was purchased by the City of St. Catharines in the 1880s.

Perhaps referring to the English public house, hotel or bar ("a drink on the house"), "House" is used in conjunction with the early development of "hotels" and tourist-related facilities at the falls: **Bath House, Cataract House, Clifton House, Prospect House** and **Table Rock House. Stephenson House** and **Welland House** helped St. Catharines develop in the mid-nineteenth century as a spa resort in conjunction with its mineral springs.

With over 200 cemeteries in the Niagara Region, many pioneers are commemorated in their "stones of history". An example is the **Warner Cemetery,** Niagara-on-the-Lake, where Christian Warner, first leader of the Methodist Congregation, is buried, and now a designated historic site. Others include the **Haynes, Honsinger, Hotstetter-Cook, May, McCombs, Schram-Tinlin** and **Ten Broeck** cemeteries in St. Catharines. Every community can add to this brief selection, and the subject provides scope for a volume in its own right.

At Ridgeville the **Dawdy-Beckett Cemetery** has been changed to **Hillside Cemetery. Eden Cemetery** in the Town of Lincoln is not a family name, but refers to the biblical "Garden of Eden". Probably once called **Mount Hope** (a name intended for the cemetery in St. Catharines), the **Mennonite Mountain Burial Ground** at Campden is where the grandparents of former Governor General Roland Michener are buried. A Presbyterian cemetery in Clinton Township was named **Mount Pleasant** in 1824. Its church, the **Good Will Meeting House,** was in 1870 referred to as **Mount Pleasant Church.**

Women's names are not forgotten when naming the landscape.

FEMALE NAMES

Of course, not all settlers were men, and their womenfolk are frequently commemorated. **St. Catharines** is named after the daughter of John Askin and his Indian wife. Askin was a prominent Detroit merchant with close Montreal connections. Catherine, educated in a convent at Montreal, in 1778 married Samuel Robertson, the captain of an Upper Lakes sailing vessel. After his death in 1782, she married Robert Hamilton in 1784, gave birth to five sons and died in 1796. Hamilton, a prosperous merchant at Queenston on the Niagara Portage whose son gave his name to **Hamilton**, owned extensive tracts of land in St. Catharines including a mill and a warehouse on Twelve Mile Creek; he gave land for the first church and school in the community.

The possibility of a name after the wife of either John Butler or Hamilton Merritt has been disavowed. Though confusing, the correct official spelling is now St. Catharines, though both the early post office and the later Grand Trunk Railway used St. Catherines. The Roman Catholic Cathedral, dedicated to St. Catherine of Alexandria, patron saint of Malta, adds a note of confusion. Another difficulty is that St.

Catharines Collegiate has an address on Catherine Street!

St. Anns is named after Ann Snyder (née Frease). Adam Snyder, who owned a grist mill, came to Niagara from New Jersey. **Snyders Mills** was renamed **St. Anns** after his wife, who befriended Indians and was regarded by them as a saint. Another saintly provision is **St. Mary's**, later **Bridgeport**, now **Jordan Station**.

Whether the name is male or female, the saintly prefix bestows a certain air of dignity upon a place. As Junius (1856) remarked in his introduction to **Saint Catharines:** "if a good **name** avail anything (and who is there, that don't believe in the virtue of a proper name) then our **saintly named town** deserves particular notice, special regard and suitable attention from all." Saint in this instance, perhaps for emphasis, was written out in full.

White Pigeon near Snyder invites the pleasing supposition that it could be named after an innkeeper's daughter who always dressed in white. A name after a local landowner, Captain Weisshuhn (White Hen), is also a possibility. **Weisshuhn's Point,** at the junction of Lyons Creek with the Welland River, was the site of a battery erected during the War of 1812.

ETHNIC NAMES

Names often indicate an ethnic group. The waves of Germanic speaking Mennonite immigrants to Lincoln are reflected in **Albright Gardens** after the Albright (Albrecht) family, **Dutch Lane** refers to Pennsylvania-German settlers, as do roads and streets named **Claus, Culp, Dobrindt, Edelheim, Fretz, Moyer** and **Tufford.** Amos Albright and Abram Moyer were the leaders who in 1799 purchased 1,100 acres (445.1 ha) of land near Twenty Mile Creek to settle their group from Pennsylvania. Known as the **Pennsylvania Dutch,** they were actually German, Dutch being an incorrect anglicization of "deutsch". **Moyer's Corners,** renamed **Campden** in 1862 when a post office was established, could reflect British associations. Gainsborough is a town in Lincolnshire and the Earl of Gainsborough was known as Viscount Campden.

Bismarck, named after the Prussian statesman and general, was founded in 1830 by Christian Sunday from Germany. He taught the German language in school, sang in German at church, and gave his name to **Sunday's Settlement.** It became **Ball's Corner** in 1860 when Crysler Ball was a storekeeper, and **Bismarck** as a post office name from 1872 on.

Immigration to Willoughby and Bertie Townships included German-speaking settlers from Alsace, who arrived in the Niagara Peninsula during the 1830s and 1840s via New York City and the Erie Canal. **Snyder,** initially **Ortville (Ort Road** still exists) but known locally as **New Germany** after its inhabitants, is one outcome. When a post office opened, this was named after Rev. T. Snyder, the Lutheran minister who promoted its achievement. **Snyder** in turn became the name of the village when its name was changed to avoid anti-German hostility, though **New Germany** is still used locally. "New", a prefix as in **Nova Scotia** or **New England,** appears to be a wish to embody the old country in a new land.

The various faiths represented at Niagara include Lutheran churches established in Willoughby Township. The Mennonite influx after American Independence is remembered by naming rural roads after **Beam** (Boehm) and **Bossert,** while **Weinbrenner, Winger** and **Sherk** are Tunker names, and the later German-Alsatian immigration of the 1830s is commemorated by road names such as **Detenbeck** (Dietenbech), **Morningstar** (Morgenstern), **Miller** (Müller), **Nye** (Nigh), **Ort** (Orth), **Weaver** (Weber) and **Willick** (Willich). Here in the southeast rural quadrant of Niagara is a rich and staunch reminder of lanscape as biography.

Quaker Township was an early name for the area renamed **Crowland Township** by Lieutenant Governor Simcoe. Likewise, **New Holland** is an earlier name for the Allanburg area, presumably because many of the pioneer settlers were of Dutch or German origin; a lesser possibility

Creeks named by distance from the Niagara River, a drawing by Mrs. Simcoe.

is some link with Samuel Johannes Holland, a surveyor who played a prominent role in shaping the new country. **Winger** is after the first postmaster, Jacob Winger. As a contrast in ethnicity, David Morgan of **Morgans Point** (not Morgan Point, but previously **Point Industry**) was a Welsh immigrant, and **Torosian Park,** St. Catharines, is in memory of that Armenian family.

A French name with many variants belongs to the early Huguenot settler who is known to have signed his name **DeCou** on muster roll, but found his name spelled and pronounced in several ways: **DeCou, DeCoo** and **DeCow.** The entry in the **Dictionary of Canadian Biography** is under **DeCow,** but **DeCew** is the spelling used by the family. The Niagara Peninsula prefers to remember him as **DeCew**, as at **DeCew Falls**, the **DeCew Campus** of Brock University or **DeCew Road.**

Other cultural groups who played a part in early settlement include Blacks. Canadian settlers were allowed to bring in slaves, but an Act of 1793 made children born to a slave mother free at the age of twenty-five. After the turn of the nineteenth century, most Blacks were free. They could own land, farm it in their own right and work as tradesmen, which in turn led to a movement out from the United States by the "underground railroad", an informal network of people and places that helped fugitive slaves to escape from the southern slave states. Richard Pierpoint, not an escaped slave but a disbanded Butler's Ranger, settled in St. Catharines. He gave his name to **Dick's Creek,** part of the route to be followed by the First Welland Canal, and is honoured by an historical plaque in the area now called **Canal Valley.**

Little Africa, an early Black settlement on the outskirts of Fort Erie, supplied wood fuel for railway locomotives. **Slabtown,** named for the shanties built with the useless timber siding of trees cut for lumber, denoted a poor community; usually associated with Merritton, it was also applied to a community of poor Black families near Chippawa. Drummondville, now part of Niagara Falls, had a district known as **Pollytown** after a man named Polly who helped Blacks settle in the area. In St. Catharines the area around North Street was known as the **Coloured Village.** At Niagara, Blacks lived on Mary Street, and McNab Point on Lake Ontario was also known as **Nigger Point.** There is a plaque at Niagara-on-the-Lake commemorating the **Negro Burying Ground,** 1830.

The Facer Street area of present day St. Catharines, once separated from the main urban area by the Third Welland Canal, was known as **Little Europe. Little Armenia** developed close to the General Motors plant on Ontario Street, where many of this group worked in the foundries after fleeing from Turkish massacres during the First World War.

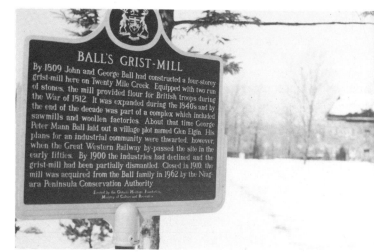

Naming the landscape after a pioneer is a typical feature of the Niagara area.

RELIGIOUS, CLASSICAL AND LITERARY NAMES

Jordan is a name of uncertain origin. One possibility is that the religious Mennonite groups compared crossing the steep-sided valley of Twenty Mile Creek to crossing the River Jordan into "the promised land". As a group with their own customs settling new territory, they were able to give a significant biblical name to their village, and thereby provide Niagara with an uncharacteristic name.

Ebenezer, north of Fort Erie on the Niagara River, provides the reminder of the Ebenezer Society, a communal religious group who lived here from 1842 to 1849. **Sodom Road,** and a former **Gomorrah Road,** may be biblical descriptions protesting the former difficulties of travelling across Willoughby Marsh on inadequate roads.

Virgil and **Homer** are unique for their classical ancestry, and may be post office names used to standardize the variety of local appellations. **The (Upper) Four** or **Four Mile Creek,** then **Cross Roads (Crossroads),** then **Lawrenceville** after George Lawrence, a Methodist preacher and an adjacent landowner, became **Virgil** in 1862 after the Roman poet. **Homer,** named in 1859 after the epic Greek

Two railway stations named after their associated community.

poet, was previously **The Ten, Upper Ten,** and **Ten Mile Creek.** These names could represent an extension of the classical tradition in New York State, where both names occur in conjunction with places such as Rome, Utica and Syracuse, or be associated with the classical revival movement in architecture. The classical allusion did not spread significantly elsewhere across the international boundary into Canada.

It is intriguing that an authenticated post office existed at **Ariadne** near Beamsville from 1863 to 1868, but apparently no records of this place exist. The name could be from Greek mythology, after the daughter of Minos who provided the thread for Theseus to escape from Minotaur's labyrinth. The name is euphonious, but who was trying to escape, and from whom or what?

PREFIXES AND SUFFIXES

It has been suggested that the saintly prefix has been used for men and women of acknowledged importance. Was it to draw attention to the kind personality of the person involved or, as saint names were common in Nova Scotia, does it reflect the cultural transfer from that region of a substantial British tradition from that province? It might also be noted that saint names prevail more in Ontario than in New York State.

Further ambivalence arises through the use of the possessive 's' denoting 'of'. **St. Catharines** appears never to have been **St. Catharine's** though **St. Davids** has been **St. David's** and may be written **St. David.** With or without the apostrophe, the 's' is possessive and not the plural form. The explanation is presumably laxity in spelling and a lack of appreciation for the niceties of the English language.

The modern situation of no apostrophe is influenced by map making and the need for conformity. As early as 1924, the Geographic Board of Canada declared that possessive names should be avoided and, if retained, the apostrophe should be dropped. Later modifications permit the genitive apostrophe to be approved, but only if this is well established in local usage as in **Lundy's Lane.** Not subject to this decree, church names retain the apostrophe 's'; for example it is **St. Alban's, St. Barnabas', St. John's** and **St. George's.**

It is interesting to speculate on the suffix **-ville** to

Bridgeburg arose at the western entrance to the International Bridge.

denote a village or town. Examples referring to people include **Davidsville,** later St. Davids; **Lawrenceville,** later Virgil; **Drummondville,** later Niagara Falls; **Smithville; Stevensville; Hagersville; Dunnville;** and **Merrittsville, later Welland. Centreville,** later Merritton, is locational; **Temperanceville,** later Fonthill, and **Ridgeville** are descriptive. As "ville" is the French word for town, could a French association be involved, as at **St. Davids** where David Secord (Sicard) was a French Huguenot, or at Decewsville, founded by the Huguenot Decew when he left Niagara? Though possible, a more likely explanation is simply the aura of prestige and emphasis that ville conveys,

perhaps involving the transfer of this ending from the United States by migrating Loyalists. Many -ville suffixes occur in New York State.

The **-burg** suffix used at **Bridgeburg** which became Fort Erie, **Allanburg,** and **Butlersburg,** which became Niagara-on-the-Lake, probably carries the same explanation of prestige and emphasis, and may also be an American import. Less probable is a source related to the French villages known as "bourgs" or "faubourgs" which had developed in the seigneuries of Quebec. The **-borough** endings for **Canborough** and **Gainsborough** may follow the same argument of prestige.

5.
Consolidation And Expansion: The Welland Canals

The Welland Canal transformed the pioneer ethos of the Niagara Peninsula. It added its structured features of channels and locks, created ports and harbours, and its flow of water could be diverted into raceways to power mill machinery. Its ships created a demand for towing operations, and for the repair and construction of vessels. Chandlers retailed supplies and equipment, and customs points, toll houses, wharves and lock keepers' cottages served the flow of passing ships. Ships' crews provided seasonal employment. Inland centres along the line of the canal grew apace, and these inducements to the growth of settlement were expanded as new canal systems were added to the landscape. This grand story of change, challenge and achievement added a myriad of new names to the pioneer toponymy.

ENGINEERING NAMES

Most Canadian canals are named after an associated place, as at **Chambly, Lachine** and **Sault Ste. Marie.** By this argument the **Welland Canal** should have been named the **Niagara Canal,** for its essential purpose was to bypass the turbulent mid-section of the Niagara River. The **Welland Canal** is however named after the Welland River, even though it neither tapped this expected source of water supply, nor used it for canal purposes as had been the intention when the **Welland Canal Company** was formed in 1824. Difficulties during the construction phase caused many of the proposed details to be changed, but left intact the name **Welland Canal** as a curious anomaly of history.

Canal refers to either a man-made waterway or an artificially improved river. When the **Welland Canal** opened in 1829, its route south from the Niagara Escarpment was in the former category, and the canalization of Twelve Mile Creek took advantage of a natural waterway. Much has changed over the years. The usual nomenclature is now the **First (Welland) Canal,** completed in 1829; the **Second (Welland) Canal,** completed in 1845; and the **Third (Welland) Canal,** completed in 1887.

Surviving lengths of the abandoned channel are mostly called the **Old Canal. Abandoned Channel** means that it no longer serves as a through route for purposes of navigation. It may however still be used for activities that include water supply, water sports, recreation, ship repair and salvage operations.

The present canal, completed in 1932, was referred to as the **Welland Ship Canal** from 1932 to 1959. The "ship" addition to distinguish it from the previous canals may stem from the Manchester Ship Canal, England. It is now generally referred to as the **Welland Canal** by its operating agency, the federal **St. Lawrence Seaway Authority,** though technically, it is the **Fourth Welland Canal.** The plural, referring to the series of canals that have crossed the Peninsula, is used by canal organizations such as the **Welland Canals Foundation,** the **Welland Canals Society** and the **Welland Canals Preservation Association.**

Each successive phase of canal development and its advancing technology have brought new names into the landscape. At the **Deep Cut** between Allanburg and Port Robinson, the First Canal was carved deeply through morainic deposits. The intention had been to tunnel through the ridges and excavate to the depth of the Welland River, but the muscles of men and animals were insufficient to undertake the required works. Landslides also resulted when spoil heaped on the banks was saturated by rain. The canal had to be constructed at a higher level than originally planned, and its water obtained from the alternative source of the Grand River when the Welland River could not be tapped.

A double-track **Railway Incline** worked by a capstan was intended at DeCew Falls for the First Canal to surmount the Niagara Escarpment, but this project had to be abandoned in favour of locks further east when the depth of the canal was increased from four to eight feet (1.2 to 2.4 m) to compete more effectively with the American Erie Canal.

When locks are constructed on a river or cut, their upper gates and the accompanying weirs control the water level above. A "pond" may develop behind the regulating weir or lock. **Martindale Pond,** the upper harbour at Port Dalhousie, formed behind the weir constructed near the harbour entrance for the Second Welland Canal. John Martindale owned land on the town line between Louth and Grantham townships. He also subscribed to canal shares, and owned a tavern in Port Dalhousie. Martindale Pond was **Asylum Basin,** asylum in the sense of a place offering protection and safety, during the period of the First Canal.

The world-famous **Royal Canadian Henley Regatta,** held annually since 1904 on the sheltered course of Martin-dale Pond, is named after the river regatta held at Henley-on-Thames, Oxfordshire, England, since 1839. The local course passes **Henley Island,** with its clubhouse and storage sheds for the rowing shells.

Marlatt's Pond and **Marlatts Road** at Beaver Dams refer to George Marlatt who owned 200 acres (80.9 ha) of land in Thorold Township. Interestingly enough, he opposed the construction of the canal as it would flood his land, create stagnant water and cause disease. The pond was also known as **Shriner's** or **Coniagas Pond. Goose Island,** a man-made island next to the Second Canal in Merritton, is named as once being a refuge for flocks of these water birds.

Ramey or **Ramey's Bend,** Port Colborne, where earlier canals made a sharp turn, was straightened when the Welland Canal By-Pass was constructed. The Ramey family, early settlers from Pennsylvania, held a land grant and owned a mill in the vicinity.

The **Feeder Canal** supplied water to the First Canal from the Grand River. It crossed the Wainfleet Marsh from Dunnville to Port Robinson, and was also used for navigational purposes. The length from Port Robinson to Welland became part of the **First Canal,** and was so called when the canal was extended south to Port Colborne in 1833. The canal then had two northern routes, to the Grand River and to Lake Erie.

The shortened Feeder Canal supplied water to the canal summit at Welland. Water then flowed north and south from this high point of the canal system. It performed this function until 1881, when the canal's depth was increased to obtain water directly from Lake Erie. The Feeder Canal, then abandoned as a source of water supply, retained a marginal navigational role for several years. The name now refers only to the stagnant length between Dunnville and Welland.

The Feeder Canal crossed the Welland River by a wooden aqueduct. This project and nearby excavation of the channel spawned a settlement of labourers. Originally known as **The Aqueduct,** the community changed its name

The Feeder Canal, west from Stromness.

The Flight Locks, the Fourth Welland Canal, the St. Lawrence Seaway Authority, and the names of the vessels and their companies are a testament to great marine engineering achievements.

to **Merrittsville** in 1842, then **Welland** in 1858. The Second Canal boasted a stone aqueduct, now a restored historical monument in a landscaped setting; **Aqueduct Street** is nearby.

The **Welland Canal By-Pass** refers to the new section of canal constructed around Welland to avoid a winding and narrow course through this city. Sometimes described as the beginning of the **Fifth Welland Canal,** this channel opened in 1973. The abandoned length of the Fourth Canal no longer functions as a commercial waterway. It has been developed and is designated as a **Recreational Waterway** with various boating regattas, sporting events and landscaped banks.

Material excavated from a canal channel has to be deposited somewhere, which in turn creates new landscape features. **Mud Lake** north of Port Colborne, developed on spoil from the Fourth Canal, is now a conservation site and a locale for the study of bird life, the **Mud Lake Wildlife Management Area.**

LOCKS AND MILLS

Canal locks have played an important role in land development. In conjunction with their potential for water power and the opportunities for trade, they have nurtured a series of canal-oriented communities. The outcome, the **Welland Canals Corridor** of development, now enmeshes the adjacent cities of St. Catharines, Thorold, Welland and Port Colborne. Each city has in turn incorporated earlier canal nodes: **Port Dalhousie** and **Merritton** in St. Catharines; **Allanburg** and **Port Robinson** in Thorold; **Welland Junction** in Welland; and **Stonebridge (Humberstone)** in Port Colborne.

Lift Locks enable boats to pass from one canal level to

49

another. They have been reduced in number, from forty on the First Canal to seven on the modern system. On each system they have been named by using sequential numbers from north to south; **Lock 1** of the present canal is on Lakeshore Road, St. Catharines, **Lock 2** on Carlton Street in the same city, and Lock 3 is south of the Queen Elizabeth Way. **Locks 4, 5 and 6** together comprise the **Flight Locks**. **Lock 7** east of Thorold is the last of the lift locks.

The set of locks known as the **Flight Locks**, a series of three interconnnected double locks to permit two-way navigation, are often compared to a "flight of stairs" and ships are said to "climb the mountain". There is also the romantic nuance of flight itself from one elevation to another. On the Second Canal, the locks along Bradley Street that surmounted the escarpment were nicknamed **Neptune's Staircase**, Neptune in Roman mythology being the god of the sea. Whether there is a link to Neptune's Staircase on the Caledonian Canal at Fort William, Scotland, is unknown.

Lock 8, at the Port Colborne entrance to the canal, is a **Guard Lock** which protects the canal from varying water levels in Lake Erie. The impression given of eight locks along the canal is misleading. If each of the three Flight Locks arranged in sets of two is counted as an individual lock, the modern Welland Canal has eleven locks.

Lock names enter the community consciousness. The favoured viewing areas of the modern canal are at **Lock 3**, St. Catharines, the **Flight Locks** and **Lock 8**, Port Colborne. **Lock 7 Motel** overlooks the canal in Thorold. **Locks 1, 2 and 8** support road bridges. Port Dalhousie, Thorold, Welland and Port Colborne have **Lock Streets,** and St. Catharines a **Lockview School.**

The difference in water levels at the locks on the first two canals was about eight feet (2.4 m). Millraces, the fast-flowing stream of water used to drive mill wheels, might use this water diverted from the canal as power potential to drive machinery. The most important of such endeavours, operated by a partnership known as the **Hydraulic Company**, took water from the First

Bridges along the Welland Canal are numbered from north to south, as are the locks.

and then the Second Canal near Merritton. This flow was fed along the top of the canal's eastern bank to St. Catharines. **Hastings Street,** named after Thomas F. Hastings, a Mayor of Merritton, was **Race Street** until 1888.

Dignified by the name of **Hydraulic Raceway** after the company, a tier of millraces followed the contours of the bank below St. Paul Street. Their mills promoted St. Catharines rapidly from a local agricultural centre to a major industrial town soon after the advent of the First Canal in 1829. When this hydraulic system was drained, **Race Street** was constructed along the route of the former hydraulic channel to provide a well-named reminder of this important industrial water system. Nearby **Head Street** may refer to a head of water, though a different interpretation will later be suggested.

At Thorold, raceways and ponds took advantage of the locks and sloping land to service many industrial establishments near the town centre. Industrial buildings rather than names survive. The **Welland Raceway,** completed in 1888, allowed this city to have its first electric plant and waterworks. The latter, being unfiltered and unchlorinated, introduced a typhoid epidemic in 1912.

THE CANAL PORTS AND CENTRES

Vessels towed through the early canals by horses and one used a towpath on the west bank. **Towpath Road,** Thorold, provides the reminder of this early canal feature. **Front Street,** Thorold, is so named because it faced the canal, as was **Front Street,** Port Dalhousie, until the name was changed to **Lakeport.**

After the introductory sod-turning ceremony in 1824, the participants repaired to the **Black Horse Inn** for a good dinner. Now demolished, the name survives in **Black Horse Corners** east of Allanburg. Controversial in meaning, the name may refer to either the ownership of a magnificent black horse, or be a name given by Dutch settlers because it appeared frequently on the inn signboards in Holland.

The "Port" prefix to a place name is used at former customs points of entry to the canal system, and where harbours for receiving and unloading cargoes connected with other systems of movement. **Port Dalhousie** and **Port Colborne** developed as ports of entry to the Welland Canal from Lake Ontario and Lake Erie. Port Colborne retains this feature whereas Port Dalhousie, the port for the first three canals, has been displaced by **Port Weller** on the Fourth Canal. **Port Robinson** arose at the southern end of the **Deep Cut** where locks connected with the lower Welland River en route to the Niagara River at Chippawa, and **Port Maitland** developed at the mouth of the Grand River with access to the Feeder Canal and navigation along the Grand River.

The centres that emerged along the canal were named by William Hamilton Merritt after dignitaries who had supported the canal venture. **Allanburgh** (now **Allanburg**) is named after William Allan, first President of the Bank of Upper Canada and Vice-President of the Welland Canal Company; the "burg" suffix could refer to John Vanderburgh, one of the first settlers and a name still to be found in this village. **Dunnville** memorialized the Hon. John Henry Dunn, Receiver General of Upper Canada in 1824, Presi-

dent of the Canal Company and a major shareholder.

Gravelly Bay became **Port Colborne** to honour Sir John Colborne, Lieutenant Governor of Upper Canada from 1828 to 1836. Now part of Port Colborne, **Humberstone** was formerly **Stonebridge,** then **Peterburgh (Petersburg)** after Peter Neff; **Neff Street** survives to recall this early settler of German descent via Pennsylvania; Humberstone is both a township and later a post office name.

Port Maitland at the mouth of the Grand River was named in honour of Sir Peregrine Maitland, Lieutenant Governor of Upper Canada from 1818 to 1828. **Port Dalhousie** (previously **The Harbour**) recalled Sir George Ramsay, the 9th Earl of Dalhousie, and Governor General of Canada from 1819 to 1828. The residents of "Port" know that Dalhousie University, Halifax, gives full solemnity to the name of the same founder. Even so, by some curious disregard for formality, the name is articulated in Niagara as "Daloozie", an historically inaccurate but distinctive local pronunciation.

Port Beverley, which became **Port Robinson,** first used the Christian name and then the surname of John Beverley Robinson, Chief Justice of Upper Canada from 1829 to 1862 and a Director of the Welland Canal Company. The **Family Compact** of officials who dominated Upper Canada until the 1830s is certainly well represented by the place names that arose across the Niagara Peninsula in conjunction with its canal achievement.

Navigation along the Welland River is indicated by the port suffix in the explicit **Wellandport. Candasville,** previously **Port Fanny,** is named after Candas Snure. **Port Davidson,** at the head of river navigation, is after a hotel owned by Alex Davidson at the junction of Diltz and Canboro Roads. **Dunnville,** first named **Grand River Dam,** is where water was diverted into the Feeder Canal from the Grand River. **Helmsport,** with its vision of turning the helm of a vessel to port, may be a misspelling for **Hellemsport** after C.W. Hellems, who ran a planning establishment in St. Catharines in 1856, but was born in Crowland Township.

The names of canal communities have often changed over time or through amalgamations to provide a confusing sequence of canal names. **Slabtown** at Elm-Oakdale Streets, **Protestant Hill** at Phelps-Turner Streets, **Centreville** at Moffatt Street, and **Westport** at Bradley-Mountain Streets became **Merritton** through the intermediate names of **Little Manchester,** then **Welland City. Welland** has evolved from **Seven Mile Stake** and **Burgess,** through **The Aqueduct** to **Merrittsville.** There has been an almost direct reversal of names between **Welland City** which became **Merritton,** and **Merrittsville** which became **Welland,** a rare toponymic feature. On the feeder canal, **Broad Creek** became **Stromness,** and **Marshville** has foregone its uncomplimentary swampy title for **Wainfleet.**

Merritton, currently a ward of St. Catharines, now provides the only direct reminder in terms of canal place names for Merritt's capable business acumen. Subsidiary names include the **Merrittville Highway** to Welland from Brock University and **Merritt Streets** in each of the cities along the canal. The **Merritt Trail (Merrittrail),** a bicycle and walking trail, now follows the canal from Port Dalhousie to Port Colborne.

In Welland, **Merritt Island**, created in 1932 but named in 1979, lies between the abandoned Fourth Canal and the Welland River; and **Merritt Park** is located on a site formerly occupied by **McCarthy's Pond,** named after Dennis McCarthy who helped to dig the Welland Canal. Though Merritt had taken precedence because of his renowned position, names recalling the Irish labour force of construction workers might usefully have been retained out of social and cultural recognition for their contributions to the canal works.

The canal itself, and mainly the First Canal, was irreverently called **Merritt's Ditch,** akin to **Clinton's Ditch** for the American Erie Canal. But as cynicism about Merritt's "crazy crotchet", also referred to as "the little brook" or "Boat Canal", changed to praise for a successful venture, it was applauded by phrases such as "the big highway Ship Canal".

HONORABLE WILLIAM HAMILTON MERRITT

The Niagara Peninsula's most famous personality was the initiator and promoter of the Welland Canal enterprise.

Oak Hall, now the CKTB radio station for St. Catharines but the former home of William Hamilton Merritt, is presumed to be named after oak trees on the property. In 1981 the Standard Broadcasting Corporation announced that the radio station would be renamed **The William Hamilton Merritt Broadcasting House,** but this promotional concept offering the possibility of acclaim for a local entrepreneur described as "The Father of Canadian Transportation" was not pursued when the station changed its ownership. A new branch of the St. Catharines Public Library is named the **William Hamilton Merritt Branch,** and the **Merritt Building** is part of the Welland Campus of the Niagara College of Applied Arts and Technology.

Calvin (Calvin Phelps), **Keefer, Phelps** and **Yates**

Portrait of a name — Henry Shickluna, son of the famous Louis Shickluna.

Streets are named after leaders and promoters of the canal endeavours. **Yates Street,** St. Catharines, is after the New York entrepreneur, John B. Yates, who purchased the right to sell or lease surplus canal water and who founded the Hydraulic Company. About 1830 the **Welland Canal Loan Company** purchased an extensive area in Merritton to develop water power from the Welland Canal for industrial purposes. Saw mills, cotton mills, foundries and paper mills resulted.

Shickluna Street recalls Louis Shickluna (or Shickeluna) and his shipyard, located in the area below the present day Burgoyne Bridge, St. Catharines. Described in 1856 as "the largest boat builder in Canada..., Mr. S. Boats... will outride any storm, surmount any stress of weather, overcome any difficulty, carry a big load and ride safely into Port." Shickluna, an immigrant from Malta via the United States, purchased his yard in the early 1840s. It was active until 1879, producing sailing and steam vessels. It employed a variety of skilled craftsmen, including carpenters renowned for the quality of their work. **Henrietta Street** is after Henrietta (née Hainer) Shickluna, and **Victoria Street** should have been **Vittoria,** after a Shickluna child. **Rebecca, Permilla, Ambrose** and **Henry Streets** are named after other members of the Shickluna family.

Port Weller, the artificial harbour at the entrance to the modern canal, is named after J.L. Weller, Superintending Engineer for constructing the Fourth Canal from 1907 to 1912, then Engineer-in-Charge from 1913 to 1917. The alternatives of **Port Muir** or **Muirsport** after a local landowner were not accepted, but James Jones, the original Loyalist grantee of the lot on which Port Weller is situated, survives in **Jones Beach. Weller Park** was previously **Garden City Beach.** The Muir possibility related to the Muir brothers of the Muir Dry Dock, Port Dalhousie, with the Port Weller Dry Docks being a continuation of that enterprise after the opening of the Fourth Canal.

Port Colborne, with links to the Welland Canal since 1833, expresses this long term association with streets named after William Hamilton **Merritt** and his wife **Catharine.** The division between **East** and **West Main Streets** is at the former Third Canal, and **East** and **West Streets** once existed on both sides of the canal south of Clarence Street; East Street was acquired and wiped out for widening the channel of the present Canal. Further canal associations include streets after A.J. **Grant,** appointed Chief Engineer of the Welland Ship Canal in 1919; Hamilton H. **Killaly,** appointed Engineer of the Welland Canal and Inspector of Railways in 1859; and George **Keefer,** the first President of the Welland Canal Company in 1823.

In Thorold, the now infilled route of the Second Canal divides **Albert Street East** from **Albert Street West.** In Welland, the abandoned Fourth Canal divides the eastern and western sections of **Main** and **Lincoln Streets.** These

Pleasure crafts docked near the canal bridges at Port Colborne.

changes in name as the canal is crossed suggest that its channels, ponds and raceways provided an effective divide within the urban environment.

Today's names along the several routes of the Welland Canal bring to mind various aspects of the canal's history — canal engineers, people like Merritt and his contemporaries who were the entrepreneurs and financiers of the First Canal, landowners along the route, and engineering features such as bridges and locks. They together help to provide a distinctive toponymy for the **Welland Canals Corridor.**

6.
Marine
Niagara

Niagara, distant from the sea and an inland region of North America, has always had a rich marine component in its names because of its situation on the Niagara River, the bounding lakes and through its succession of Welland Canals. They add considerably to the land-based names that appear on maps and signs, and provide a considerable tourist asset as visitors and marine enthusiasts view the parade of passing vessels on the Welland Canal.

THE NAMES OF VESSELS

A ship's name is displayed at the bow of the vessel, at the stern which also carries the port of registry often in the language of that country, and usually on nameboards on both sides of the wheelhouse. These names are diverse, and depend on the accepted practice of each shipping company. Examples are the "Algo" prefix denoting vessels owned by the **Algoma Central Railway. Algocen** neatly combines the first letters of **Algo**ma and **Cen**tral, **Algorail** the first letters of **Algo**ma and **Rail**way, and **Algoway** combines **Algo**ma with the last letters of rail**way. Algosoo** brings in the company's headquarters at Sault Ste Marie, locally called the "Soo".

The prefix "Canadian" identifies vessels of the **Upper Lakes Shipping Company,** now **ULS International. Canadian Century,** built in 1967, commemorates Canada's centennial, and **Canadian Progress** is taken from the motto of this centennial year, "A Century of Progress". River names such as **Saguenay** or **Richelieu** indicate rivers where the ships trade. Vessels with personal names often indicate senior officers of the company, for example **Ralph Misener** or **Scott Misener** of the Misener Shipping Company.

Port Weller Dry Dock, a subsidiary of ULS International, built the Canadian series identified above. With their date of construction in brackets, other vessels have been named after company officers, for example the **James Norris** (1952), **Gordon C. Leitch** (1952) and **R. Bruce Angus** (1951) whose namesake sailed the company's first ship. The **Seaway Queen** (1959) coincided with the opening of the St. Lawrence Seaway by Queen Elizabeth II. **Red Wing** (1944) was named after the Detroit hockey team, owned by Bruce Norris, a director and part owner of the company. The **Cape Breton Miner** (1964) and **Ontario Power** (1965), as indicated by their names, were built to carry coal from the mines of Nova Scotia to the generating stations of Ontario Hydro on Lake Ontario. **Imperial Acadia** denotes that this vessel was built for the Imperial Oil Company.

The N.S.&T. affectionately known as "Never Starts on Time".

The naming of vessels provides a distinctive set of names for the Niagara Peninsula.

The almost 4,000 vessels that passed through the Welland Canal in 1987 brought a veritable sea of names into the local vocabulary. The most frequent, with the number of transits in parenthesis, were **H.M. Griffiths,** (111) **J.W. McGiffin** (78), **Canadian Century** (59), **Canadian Olympic** (58) and **Canadian Progress** (50).

Foreign vessels, known amiably as "Salties" in contrast with the "Lakers" that operate on the Great Lakes, also ply the canal. Regular traders by their flag of registry include such exotic names as **Akranes** (Iceland), **Eglantine** (St. Vincent), **Krisla** (Finland), **Petka** (Yugoslavia) and **Soren Toubro** (India).

HISTORIC NAMES

Certain names are part of Niagara's long-time marine history. Off Port Dalhousie are the famed sunken American warships **Hamilton** and **Scourge,** sent to the bottom by a sudden squall during the War of 1812. Vessels with names from Niagara were used by the British naval service on the Great Lakes; they include **Brock,** built in 1817, and **Niagara** and **Queenston,** built in 1814. The British schooner **Ann(ie) and Jane,** and the American **R.H. Broughton** are famous for the first passage through an ice-covered Welland Canal in 1829. Associated with the Second and Third Welland Canals, the **Empress of India** carried passengers from Port Dalhousie to Toronto; in the 1970s this name was used for an Indian restaurant which faced the harbour close to the vessel's former mooring point. When rail service reached Niagara in 1854, connections with the steamers **Peerless** and **Clifton** were made at Niagara and Chippawa; the next year, the **Zimmerman** joined the run to Toronto.

Shipbuilding must be recalled. The Muir brothers at Port Dalhousie in the mid-nineteenth century produced "A" vessels: **Ayr** after the Scottish shire where they had lived, **Alexander** after Alexander Muir, **Arctic, Acorn, Advance, Asia** and others. The National Harbour and Dock Company at Niagara, formed in 1830 but defunct by 1848, produced the **Transit and Queen Victoria.** The Shickluna yard, St. Catharines, produced sailing and later steam vessels with names that included **Enterprise, The Welland Canal, Pride of Canada, Welland,** and **Perseverance.**

Lakeside Park, Port Dalhousie, was served by many

vessels from Toronto. The **Lakeside** was followed by **Dalhousie City, Garden City** (scrapped in the mid-1930s), then the **Northumberland.** The latter burned in the harbour in 1949, with **Dalhousie City** surviving another year before falling victim to the rising volumes of competitive motor traffic for recreational excursions.

Of the ships that served the amusement park at Crystal Beach, the first were sidewheelers: **Dove** and **Pearl,** 1892; **Gazelle** and **Puritan,** 1894. Then came **Ossian Bedell,** named after the owner of the Bedell Hotel on Grand Island, and **Garden City** which later transferred to the Port Dalhousie-Toronto run. Built at Buffalo circa 1910, with names chosen by a special "name-the-boats" contest, were **Americana** and **Canadiana.**

In the 1920s and 1930s vessels that served the Niagara River had the names **Cayuga, Chippewa** and **Corona. Corona** refers to the sun's rays. The two other vessels are after Indian tribes, though the former was also an early naval vessel on Lake Ontario. Later vessels beginning with a "C" and ending with an "A" include **Chicora** and **Cibola,** Spanish words meaning "land of flowers" and "land of buffalo", respectively, though why this choice of Spanish names and the significance of C...A are unknown.

WARTIME SERVICE

Several interesting World War II naval associations might be noted, for many Royal Canadian warships used as escort vessels were named after Niagara's towns. **HMCS Fort Erie** was commissioned at Quebec City in 1944, and **HMCS Port Colborne** at Esquimalt, B.C., in 1943. **HMCS Niagara,** a destroyer, was one of 50 handed over by the United States in 1940 in exchange for the use of British bases such as Bermuda. The River Class frigate, **HMCS St. Catharines,** launched at Esquimalt, B.C., in 1942 is credited with destroying at least one German submarine. **HMCS Humberstone,** commissioned in 1944 at Glasgow, Scotland, was purchased by the Royal Canadian Navy in an exchange arrangement for vessels constructed in Canada. The shield of Humberstone, England, was used as the ship's badge.

Other towns, for reasons of "local preference" by the municipal council, had variations of their names assigned to naval vessels. Merritton is remembered by the Flower Class corvette named **HMCS Merrittonia,** commissioned at Quebec City in 1944. Thorold is recalled by **HMCS Thorlock,** commissioned at Midland in 1944; also engaged with submarines, she accepted the surrender of a German U-boat and escorted her to Newfoundland.

A fitting conclusion to this chapter stressing marine names is the highly appropriate name for the ferry, owned and operated by the St. Lawrence Seaway Authority, that has replaced the fallen bridge at Port Robinson. The delightful witticism of **Bridge-It** results from a contest organized by the City of Thorold. Another excellent name is **International Steam Bridge** for the railway car ferry between Fort Erie and Buffalo; the first on the Great Lakes when launched in 1857, it provided a temporary expedient named in anticipation of a bridge across the Niagara River.

7.

Railways, Hydro-Electricity And The Streetcar

Railways added a new set of features including stations, yards and bridges, especially during the 1850s and the 1870s. They were followed by the streetcar which developed an interurban system at Niagara, and which in turn relied upon hydro-electric developments for its motive power. A series of new names results from these additional factors of transportation in the landscape.

THE RAILWAY ERA

Railway companies operating in the Peninsula have changed their names and ownership over the years. The routes in current use, mostly **Canadian National** but also American **(Michigan Central)** lines of track, have their predecessors. The evidence of earlier railway names is slender, but it includes **Great Western Street** and the **Western Hill District** of St. Catharines after the **Great Western** (later **Grand Trunk**) that opened a line between Hamilton and Niagara Falls in 1853.

Michigan Avenue, Michigan Beach and the east or **Michigan Side** of the canal at Port Dalhousie probably recall the winter migration to Michigan of canal workers, jobless when the canal was closed by ice but searching for work as woodsmen. An alternative explanation is that the "Micks", a term used disparagingly for Roman Catholic labouring groups, inhabited the area.

The **Welland Railway,** which crossed the east-west lines of track at grade, gave rise to "junctions" where two railway routes crossed, for example **Allanburg Junction** and **Air Line Junction.** The latter name, redesignated **Welland Junction,** survives as part of the City of Welland. An air line is the shortest distance between any two geographical points, a direct line "as the crow flies" or a "beeline", in this instance from Detroit to the Niagara River rather than via the earlier but circuitous and longer route through Hamilton.

At Stevensville, **Airline Street** provides a reminder for the **Canada Air Line** loop of the **Great Western Railway;** an earlier name was **Hog Alley** for its use by farmers shipping their pigs to market by train. Streets named **Railway** or **Railroad** follow former lines of track in St. Catharines, Welland and Niagara-on-the-Lake, and the several **Division Streets** are probably related to the divisional organization of the railway companies. The names of railway stations in existence at 1914 are depicted in Fig. 7.1.

The Suspension Bridge, so named because the weight was carried by four ten inch (25.4 cm) cables of wrought iron wire, spanned the gorge of the Niagara River to interconnect the Canadian and American rail systems. Charters in 1846 for its construction had different names,

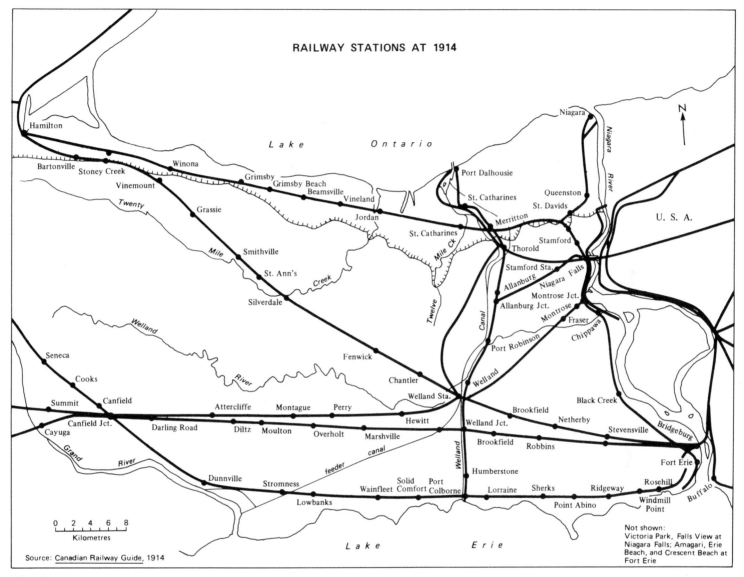

Fig. 7.1

Befitting Niagara's status as a border community, the name International signifies an important aspect of regional situation.

the **Niagara Falls International Bridge Company** from the State of New York and the **Niagara Falls Suspension Bridge Company** from the Canadian government. This variation reflects administrative differences across the intervening international boundary.

The bridge had two levels—a single track railway on the upper deck and an enclosed roadway for horse, carriage and pedestrian traffic below. It was replaced in 1897 by the **Niagara Railway Steel Arch Bridge,** constructed on the same site by building the new bridge under and into the structure of the old.

The Canadian bridgehead settlement and main line terminus was named **Elgin** in 1853, after James Bruce, 8th Earl of Elgin and 12th Earl of Kincardine, the Governor General of the period. As other places had this distinguished name, the post office was called **Suspension Bridge** from 1852 to 1857. Construction of the nearby **Niagara Cantilever Bridge** over the gorge in 1883 strengthened the Elgin-Clifton location, now part of Niagara Falls.

The **International Bridge Company** obtained charters from the State of New York and Canada to construct a bridge across the Niagara River between Waterloo (Fort Erie) and Black Rock (Buffalo). The **International Bridge** opened in 1873. The new community that arose at its western end for construction gangs, later a booming railway centre, was named **Victoria** after the reigning British monarch. To avoid confusion with other such names, the post office became **International Bridge** in 1877. The railway community became **Bridgeburg,** renamed **Fort Erie** in 1931.

Downtown Fort Erie was developed by Stephen M. Jarvis, a name recalled in **Jarvis Street,** the main shopping street that paralleled the railway track. The name for the nearby centre of **Amigari,** which also obtained a railway station, could be a misspelling. One theory is that it should have been **Amigan,** the birthplace in Limerick, Ireland, of the Hon. Christopher William Bunting, M.P. for Welland from 1878 to 1882 and later proprietor of the Toronto **Mail.** The incorrect final "ri" instead of "n" is presumably the result of post office officials misreading the handwritten name that had been suggested.

Development also occurred where the **Great Western** railway crossed Twenty Mile Creek. As a construction settlement emerged on the east bank, the small community of **St. Mary's** became **Bridgeport** then **Jordan Station** at this location. Named after the nearby older village of **Jordan,** it soon eclipsed its mentor in importance. The new community became a Police Village in 1915, but the older centre did not attain this status until 1924.

The railway, as it crossed the Ontario Plain north of the Niagara Escarpment, passed close to the established centres. It elongated these communities and mostly received their names for its stations, as at **Beamsville, Grimsby** and **St. Catharines. Jordan Station** was an exception in that a new community was added; the same event occurred at **Ontario** (later **Winona**). **Vineland Station,** established in 1910 to assist the export of fruit, also received its name from the nearby village. These names have persisted even though their stations are no longer active.

A different situation prevailed in the south of the Peninsula. Two almost parallel lines constructed during the

Vineland: An appropriate name within the Niagara Fruit Belt.

The notable station at Smithville on the T.H. & B. line.

1870s, the **Canadian Southern** and the **Great Western (Canada Air Line)**, competed for trade along the route from Detroit to Buffalo and New York. The rural population was sparse, and new station names had to be introduced along the lines of track such as **Attercliffe, Brookfield, Darling Road, Diltz** and **Hewitt.** As trains carried the mail, the station frequently attracted a post office. Singly or together, they often became a local centre of community life in rural areas.

The first postmaster had the right to name the office, and frequently awarded his name. In the south of the Peninsula, stations with post offices included **Darling Road** and **Hewitt** from 1883. "Station" is added after the name of the post office at **Attercliffe** from 1874, **Brookfield** from 1876 and at **Perry** from 1883. At **Moulton** it is included from 1877, but dropped in 1893. **Diltz, Montague, Overholt** and **Robbins** did not have a post office associated with the stations. To the south, **Sherks** was the name of the station, but the post office from 1862 was **Sherkston.**

Stations named for individuals were **Hewitt** after the school teacher, J.B. Hewitt; **Brookfield** after Emanuel Winter Brookfield, postmaster for many years; and **Sherks**

after Wilson Sherk. **Montague** is after the first station agent. Names given by the first postmaster are **Abingdon** in 1856 by Andrew Wilson; **Fulton** in 1853 by L. Greenan; **Rosedene** in 1862 at **Vienna Hamlet** by Cornelius McKay; and **Boyle** in 1887 by George Putnam. The names presumably imply some association linked with these persons; for example, **Rosedene** might refer to the roses grown by the postmaster's wife.

The tradition of post office-railway links continued when the **Toronto, Hamilton and Buffalo,** known popularly as the **T.H. & B.,** opened for operation between Hamilton and Welland in 1895, and between Toronto and Buffalo in 1897. Owned by the **New York Central** and the **Canadian Pacific,** it added stations at **Grassie, Smithville, St. Anns, Silverdale, Fenwick, Chantler, Brookfield, Netherby** and **Stevensville.** Of the new names **Grassie,** previously the **Muir Settlement** after a pioneer family, obtained a post office named after John Grassie, the first blacksmith and settler. **Fenwick,** previously **Diffin's Corners,** was a post office name, perhaps from the birthplace in Ayrshire, Scotland, of Dr. John Fraser, a reeve of Pelham.

Burnaby, established in 1885, was named after Colonel Frederic Gustavus Burnaby, an extraordinary character renowned for several expeditions through South America and Central Africa, and the first man to make the air trip from England to France in a balloon. **Attercliffe** was named by Dr. John Kirby in memory of that town in England, and **Tintern** presumably has the same British link.

Possibly John Thompson, the first or second postmaster at **Montrose,** gave the post office this name because of his connections with Montrose in Angus, Scotland. **Montrose Yards** are close to the international boundary inland from Niagara Falls. **Elcho** is presumed to be after Lord Elcho, and **Winslow** after Emerson J. Winslow, postmaster and merchant.

Moulton, a late township name for land purchased from the Six Nations Indians, was changed from **Widderburn** by the Hon. D'Arcy Boulton, Attorney General of the Province, and renamed after the family seat in Lincolnshire, England. **Canfield** (previously **Azoff,** a Russian lake), is named after a lumber merchant of the village.

RAILWAYS AND TOURISM

The **Buffalo, Brantford and Goderich Railway** which opened in 1854 became the **Buffalo and Lake Huron Railway** in 1856. Later, as part of the **Grand Trunk** system, it contributed to the expansion of American summer resort communities along the northern shore of Lake Erie. Its stations provided access to Buffalo, making commuting possible during the season. **Solid Comfort,** developed by the Humberstone Summer Resort Club west of Port Colborne in 1888, was a flag station named to reflect the ease and well-being of its associated community.

An exclusive summer retreat for gentlemen from Memphis, **Tennessee,** developed around what is today **Tennessee Avenue,** Port Colborne. **Lorraine,** east of the Welland Canal and another exclusive resort community, was named after the only daughter of Frank Fulton Brown, a Buffalo businessman who erected the first summer home there in 1898.

Only the name **Fort Erie Beach,** originally **Snake Hill Grove,** has survived from the amusement complex which once featured a casino-dance hall, athletic stadium, parks, promenades and zoo. Served by the delightfully named but over-ambitious (was it ever intended to reach the Western Ocean?) **Fort Erie, Snake Hill and Pacific Railroad,** it was better known as the **Peanut Special** or the **Sandfly Express,** excellent examples of how popular phraseology carried greater meaning than official terminology. Another example, the flippant **Paddy Miles Express** named after its witty Irish conductor, was officially the **Erie and Ontario** line between Fort Erie and Niagara.

With visitors arriving by train and boat, St. Catharines was dubbed **Saratoga of the North** in the mid-nineteenth century for its medicinal spa waters. The once-sumptuous **Welland House Hotel** recalls the promenade of wealthy visitors, as does **Springbank Drive** which faces the site of this once majestic hotel on the east side of Twelve Mile Creek.

Tourism expanded considerably at Niagara Falls due to the railways, though few of the names survive. An important station, **Victoria Park** (later **Clifton Hill**), was constructed at the top of this hill to provide easy access to the parks and falls. **Wesley Park Station** served Methodist camp meeting grounds, which became the site of the **Niagara Falls Collegiate** centred on **Epworth** and **Ryerson Circles. Falls View** or "**Inspiration Point Station**" next to **Loretto Academy** had a large viewing platform above the falls and rapids. All day trains stopped here for passengers to admire the grand panoramic overview.

The **Erie and Ontario** railway (later **Michigan Central**) helped to promote the prestigious **Queens Royal Hotel** on Front Street at King in Niagara-on-the-Lake. At first named the **Royal Niagara Hotel,** this elegant, four storey resort hotel opened in 1866 with funding from compensation received when St. Catharines usurped Niagara as the county seat for Lincoln. The hotel was demolished in 1931 and the site has become **Queens Royal Park.**

A French - Huguenot Pioneer gives his name to the DeCew Power Generating Station.

Also at Niagara-on-the-Lake, in an area known previously as **Crookston,** the **Canadian Chautauqua** developed next to Lake Ontario after 1887. Served by a spur line from a station on the **Michigan Central** railway and the docks, it opened as a summer educational and religious retreat. The name is derived from a similar resort complex developed on the lake of that name in Western New York State. The complex survived until 1909, when the central **Hotel Chautauqua** was destroyed by fire. Now known as **Mississauga Beach** the area has been developed with residential building lots. The central park has become the site of a circular road, and the names of the radial avenues recall religious reformers: **Addison, Luther, Vincent, Wilberforce, Wycliffe** and **Wesley.**

A similar arrangement exists at **Crystal Beach** and **Grimsby Beach,** each with surviving central circles. The **Crystal Beach Amusement Park,** conceived as an assembly ground for physical and mental uplift in the 1880s but a recreational resort by 1890, was served mostly by steamer and by the innovative **Ontario Southern** railway. Dubbed the **Peg-Leg Railway** as a jocular term for a railway raised above ground level on stout T-shaped oak posts, it survived for but a few years. J.E. Rebstock, founder of the resort and honoured as the "grand old man of Crystal Beach", has **Rebstock Road** in his memory.

The religious area at Crystal Beach is still evident on the ground. Centered on **Queens Circle,** the inner and outer rectangles of **Lincoln** and **Cambridge,** and the diagonal streets of **Belfast** and **Shannon,** together present a distinctive urban form. At Grimsby Beach, **Auditorium Circle, Temple Lane, Wesley Avenue, Park Road** and **Grand Avenue** survive from this summer interlude of prayer and recreation.

HYDRO-ELECTRICITY

Small power projects which took advantage of the fall of water through the abandoned locks of the Second Welland Canal often used their location, such as **Lock 3** and **Lock 5,** for identification purposes. More extensively, the **Cataract Power Company** of Hamilton was organized in 1896 to develop power at DeCew Falls. A channel was cut from the Welland Canal at Allanburg to the edge of the Niagara Escarpment at DeCew Falls, where penstocks fed the turbines of the **DeCew Generating Station.**

Three of five persons named John associated with the power company, namely John M. Gibson (President), John Patterson (Secretary) and John Moodie (Director), are commemorated in storage reservoirs named **Lakes Gibson, Patterson** and **Moodie.** Enlargements carried out after World War II have reduced the distinctiveness of once separate lakes. **Power Glen,** a suitable descriptive name for the village of the Cataract Power Company on the northwest side of Twelve Mile Creek, replaced the earlier centre of **Reynoldsville** named after Reynold's sawmill.

When hydro-electric power later developed at Niagara Falls, power stations were established on Canadian soil by American interests to serve American purposes. The name of an American company president is thereby introduced in the **William B. Rankine** or **Canadian Niagara Generating**

Station. It began operations in 1904 as **Plant No. 3** of the **Niagara Falls Power Company,** now the **Niagara Mohawk Power Corporation.** It was followed by the **Ontario Power Company** the next year in a majstic columned building of Italian Renaissance design. A Canadian enterprise, the **Electrical Development Company** (later **Toronto Power Company**) first generated power in 1906 on land reclaimed from the river north of Dufferin Islands. **Grass Island Pool** in the Niagara River, held back by the **International Control Dam,** provides a suitable level of water for power generation and also spreads the flow of water to reduce erosion.

When a series of power plants was constructed downstream to capture the greater height of falling water at the edge of the Niagara Escarpment, the project was named the **Queenston-Chippawa Power Development** after its location. It was renamed in 1950 after **Sir Adam Beck,** the first chairman of **Ontario Hydro** (originally the cumbersome **Hydro-Electric Power Commission of the Province of Ontario**), to commemorate the "father of hydroelectric power" in Ontario.

A different type of power resource, the extraction of natural gas from under Lake Erie and the southern parts of Welland County, is reflected in the name **Gasline** (not Gas Line), a community east of Port Colborne and a place name reminder of this ongoing activity.

THE STREETCAR NETWORK

An interurban streetcar or radial trolley system developed as a consequence of the local power resource. The **Niagara, St. Catharines and Toronto** railway which interlinked the eastern areas of the Peninsula enjoyed wide public use. Abbreviated to **N.S. & T.**, these letters were changed by a critical public to mean either "Naturally Slow and Tired" or "Never Starts on Time"! There was also the **International Railway Company** and its spectacular **Great Gorge Route** between Niagara Falls and Queenston-Lewiston, in the gorge on the American side of the Niagara River and along its crest on the Canadian side.

A reminder of a bygone pleasure on the praised "Most Scenic Route in North America".

The **N.S. & T.** stations included **Slater's Dock** on the Niagara River, where the trolley line was extended south from Chipppawa to serve a boat to Buffalo during the Pan-American Exposition of 1901. **Electric Park,** developed as a residential subdivision between Fonthill and Welland, became **Stop 19,** the nineteenth stop on the interurban line from Welland to Port Colborne.

Stops along the streetcar routes often took the name of the streets they followed or crossed, the major industries which they served, and local centres. Between St. Catharines and Niagara-on-the-Lake, stops were **Facer Street, Scott Street, Lake Shore, McNab, Coleman's** and **Chaplin's.** In St. Catharines **McKinnons** (now **General Motors**) and **Victoria Lawn Cemetery** gave their names to terminals that were twenty minutes apart by streetcar. **Barnesdale,** originally a stop named after Barnes Winery, has been perpetuated by a residence with that name for the mentally handicapped.

Local cars in Niagara Falls served **Bridge Street, Queen & Victoria, Newman Mill, Main & Ferry, Winery Road** and **Montrose.** On the main line to St. Catharines from **Tower Inn Terminal** were **Queen** and **Bridge Streets, Fourth Avenue** and **Stanley, Stamford** and local points of identification: **Hutt's, Kalar's, Lobbs, Town Line, Shriner's,** and **New Canal** and **Old Canal Swing Bridges.**

8.
The
Highway
Framework

From the early 1900s on, the advent of automobile and truck traffic required that roads be graded, widened and surfaced. Bridges had to be constructed over railways, streams and rivers, and routes had to be signed. New roads have been added as towns expanded and as subdivisions located in rural areas. Provincial, county, regional and municipal highway departments have together formulated and encouraged a remarkable process of landscape change. Much naming and renaming occurs as a consequence.

PROVINCIAL HIGHWAYS

To serve this increased traffic, a provincial, multi-lane highway system has evolved, remarkably different from the streets and survey roads that formerly provided access to properties along their rights-of-way (Fig.8.1). Access became restricted to irregularly-spaced junctions along the network in order to provide for the fast flow of large numbers of vehicles. These junctions are numbered from east to west consecutively in the Niagara Peninsula.

The precursor of such routes, known initially as **Middle Road** west of Toronto and as the **New Niagara Falls Highway** east from Hamilton, was named **The Queen Elizabeth Way** after the consort of King George VI when

dedicated by Her Majesty in 1939. Usually referred to in an abbreviated acronymic form as **Q.E.W.**, **QEW** or **Queen E,** at Niagara it is officially and popularly called simply the **QEW**. It is interesting to note that the later provincial highways carry a 400 numbered designation, which presumably relates to their original design feature as four-lane highways. A commemorative name may be added, as when **Highway 401** was named the **MacDonald-Cartier Freeway.**

With the QEW as the spine, the other numbered provincial highways in the Peninsula are **406** to Welland, **405** to the **Queenston-Lewiston Bridge** across the Niagara River and **420** to the **Rainbow Bridge** at Niagara Falls. All except 406 are links with the American Interstate Highway System. Interstate is abbreviated to I, with **I 90** being the New York State Thruway and **I 190** the Niagara Section of this "thruway" (an American spelling for "throughway").

Although advertising is not allowed along major provincial highways, two curious anomalies occur at Jordan Harbour. A portion of the **North Service Road** is **Beacon Boulevard** to serve this motor hotel, and **Prudhomme Boulevard** serves a motel complex named after John and George Prudhomme of Beamsville.

The numbered sequence of mostly two-lane provincial highways includes **Highway 58** and **Highway 140** in the Welland Canals Corridor. East-west are **Highway 55 (Nia-**

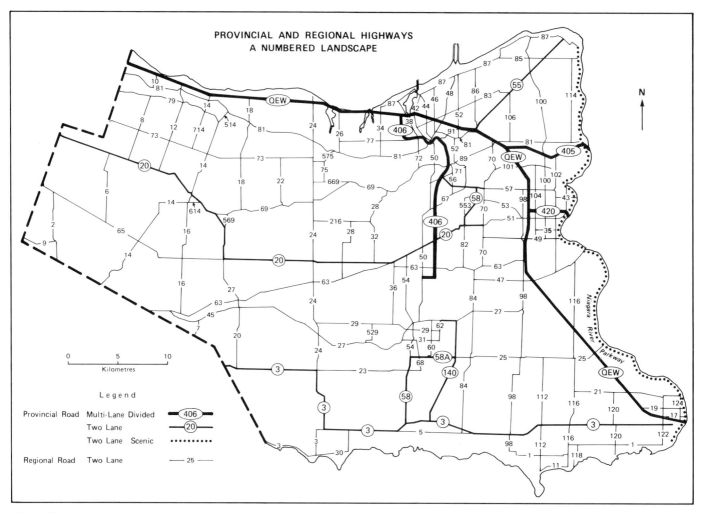

PROVINCIAL AND REGIONAL HIGHWAYS
A NUMBERED LANDSCAPE

Legend

Provincial Road   Multi-Lane Divided
                  Two Lane
                  Two Lane Scenic

Regional Road   Two Lane

Fig. 8.1

gara Stone Road) inland from Niagara-on-the-Lake, **Highway 20** (in part **Lundy's Lane**) west from Niagara Falls, and **Highway 3 (Old Garrison Road)** from Fort Erie. The latter becomes the **Talbot Trail,** a designated **Heritage Highway** to the **Talbot** settlement on the north shore of Lake Erie. Promoted by Thomas Talbot, its twenty-nine townships housed 30,000 people by the mid-1830s. In Wainfleet, **Highway 3** disrupts the continuity of names on the local north-south road system; for example, **Zion** becomes **Flanagan, Smith** becomes **Sider** and **Marr** becomes **Case** as Highway 3 is crossed.

Also under provincial auspices, but managed by the Niagara Parks Commission, is the **Niagara River Parkway** between Fort Erie and Niagara-on-the-Lake. The initial plan for the **Niagara Boulevard,** its first name, involved the removal of unsightly barriers in order to open views to the river, and the extensive planting of native and exotic trees. A world famous **Scenic Drive** has been achieved. Its excellence of design may be contrasted with the wistfully named **Robert Moses "Parkway",** the multi-lane, high-speed route on the American side.

REGIONAL HIGHWAYS

An extensive lattice of regional highways criss-crosses the Niagara Region. The intended naming scheme is that north-south highways have even numbers beginning in the west, and the east-west highways have odd numbers beginning in the south, a scheme not always followed because of changes in direction though the framework may be observed on Fig. 8.1. Elements of north-south consistency include **Highway 2 (Caistorville Road)** in West Lincoln, **Highway 24 (Victoria Avenue-Townline-Vineland)** west of the Welland Canals Corridor, and **Highway 84 (Miller-Moyer Road)** along its eastern flank. In the east-west grid **Highway 1 (Dominion Road)** extends west from Fort Erie, and **Highway 57 (Thorold Stone Road)** is west from Niagara Falls.

Highway 406 at St. Catharines: a numbered provincial route adds a new dimension to names in the modern landscape..

Before the formation of regional government, the county highways also had numbered designations. For example, **Highway 8** from Queenston to St. Catharines and Grimsby followed the bluffs of the former Lake Iroquois shoreline. The most scenic road in the Peninsula after the Niagara River Parkway, its number became so entrenched in popular imagination that **Highway 8** is still used in preference to its modern designation, **Highway 81.** Modern "consistency" has not removed the favored number from usage.

North-south roads across the Haldimand and Erie Plains to Lake Erie are frequently named after the beach, bay or headland feature on Lake Erie to which they lead: **Bertie Bay, Crescent** (Beach), **Holloway Bay, Point Abino, Prospect Point** and **Windmill Point.** This characteristic is not repeated along Lake Ontario, as the lakeshore here consists of bluffs with a more limited recreational appeal.

Numbering is used to simplify the identification of regional roads for record, maintenance and construction purposes, and to meet the requirements of the Ontario Ministry of Transportation for subsidies. It avoids the duplication of street names such as **Ontario Street,** that

The Queenston-Lewiston Bridge spans the Niagara Gorge from the Canadian side. The name is a historic transfer of its present location.

The Peace Bridge of 1927 at Fort Erie.

occur in several different municipalities and would require the renaming of such streets to eliminate repetition. As with provincial roads, it also means that the major roads have two names: an official, numbered designation, and the local street name. Numbers, convenient and orderly though they may be to the official mind and for computer analysis, nevertheless entail a regrettable loss of personal character.

Traditional and meaningful local names, rather than official numbers, are likely to survive as the common currency is use by the public. For example, **Fly Road** after "Fly" Sam Moyer for his energies and activities, seems preferable to the mundane **Regional Road 73. Regional Road 51** in Niagara Falls, itself a decisive break in the continuity of Highway 20 across the Peninsula, is better known as the named sequence of **Lundy's Lane, Ferry Street** and **Victoria Avenue.**

BRIDGES AND TUNNELS

The **Peace Bridge** at Fort Erie, the largest single crossing in terms of traffic volumes between Canada and the United States, commemorates over a century of peace along the international boundary. At its base the **Mather Arch** and **Mather Park** with its gardens are named after Alonzo C. Mather, an American businessman who fostered friendly relations between the two countries and donated towards the park and its memorial gateway.

At Niagara Falls the **Upper Steel Arch Bridge,** named for its structural characteristics, collapsed into the Niagara River in 1938 when winter ice piled up and wrenched the road bridge from its abutments. Its replacement has piers embedded in the walls of the gorge higher than any anticipated ice jam. Named the **Rainbow Bridge,** it recalls the rainbows so often seen over the falls. The road approach passes over the Niagara River Parkway, here dignified by parterre gardens, stonefaced buildings and the **Carillon Tower** with its peal of bells.

To the north, the two-decked **Whirlpool Rapids Bridge** replaced its predecessor in 1897. North again, the **Queenston-Lewiston Bridge** of 1962 replaced the **Queenston-Lewiston Suspension Bridge** that had been constructed across the entrance to the gorge between these two locations in 1899. American terminology is the **Lewiston-Queenston Bridge.** The bridge, named after the villages it formerly connected, is now distant from these two communities. Even so, the former name has been retained, though the **Queenston Heights Bridge** would be more accurate.

The QEW is taken over the Welland Canal at St. Catharines by a soaring high-level bridge to clear the masts of ships in the waterway below. Called the **Homer Skyway** during its period of construction after its location next to this village, official terminology is now the **Garden City Skyway,** an apt use of this epithet and wise advertising for St. Catharines. The **Homer Cemetery** below, one of the oldest in the peninsula, was disrupted and its Episcopal church (St. George's) replaced half a mile to the east by these road works.

More recently, tunnels have taken roadways under the Welland Canal. The **Thorold Tunnel,** opened in 1968, replaced two highway lift bridges. In Welland, **Main Street Tunnel** carries highway traffic to and from the city centre of Welland, and **Townline Tunnel** has separated "tubes" for railway and highway traffic. "Townline" refers to a location on the former boundary between Crowland and Humberstone Townships.

Road and rail bridges that cross the Welland Canal have dual names: the name of the street or railway crossing the canal, and the number allocated by canal engineers as part of the construction process. Twenty movable bridges were built. Though twenty-one had been planned, **Bridge 2** was never built. Numbered sequentially from north to south, **Bridge 1** is at Lock 1 on Lakeshore Road, St. Catharines, and **Bridge 21** is at Clarence Street, Port Colborne. Tunnels are not included in this numbered sequence because their structures do not interfere with vessel movements on the canal.

As new bridges were constructed across the canal, the suffix "A" was added. They include **Bridge 3A** at Lock 2 on Carlton Street, St. Catharines, **Bridge 4A** which is the Garden City Skyway, and **Bridge 19A** on Highway 3 in Port Colborne to bypass Lock 8. As a bridge at one or the other end of this lock is always available for highway traffic, the movement of canal vessels presents no hindrance to road movements.

The sequence of numbered bridges is complicated further by the fact that certain bridges, for example **Bridges 7, 8 and 9,** have been taken out of service and removed. Others, no longer required for canal purposes, remain in use as highway or rail crossings over the former channel. In the centre of Welland, for example, former canal bridges continue to span the abandoned channel but, in a fixed position, they no longer present points of road traffic delay. Thirteen movable highway or railway bridges now cross the canal. As three are "A" additions, only ten are survivors from the original construction works. **Bridges 6, 10 and 20** are railway bridges.

9.
The
Urban
Street System

The study of names used for roads and streets is "odonymy". As well over 1,000 named streets exist at Niagara, with frequent repetition of the same name in different municipal areas, the approach here is selective to highlight only the themes and the variety that exist.

A CHANGING NOMENCLATURE

Streets, like places, are subject to changes in their names. Fig. 9.1 provides an example from St. Catharines which, in 1961, incorporated Grantham Township and the Towns of Merritton and Port Dalhousie. Now within the same jurisdiction, the duplication of street names had necessarily to be resolved. In this process, **Church** was changed to **Linwell**, **Boyle** to **Glendale**, **Ashland** to **Bunting** and **Merrittville** to **Glenridge**, among others.

Most renaming took place at Port Dalhousie, including the loss of streets from **First** to **Ninth Avenue** and the deletion of the more common names: **Albert, Catherine, Church, Lake, Queen** and **Welland.** The village gained the poets **Keats, Masefield** and **Shelley.** It added **Pawling,** a pioneer Loyalist landowner and former Butler's Ranger, and **Muir** and **Abbey** after Scottish immigrant shipbuilders.

At Merritton, **Bradley Street** displaced Lock Street, because **Lock Street** was retained at Port Dalhousie. Bradley is deserving for he was a lockkeeper and a mayor of Merritton, though the greater historical and international significance of the unique flight locks serving the Second Welland Canal and dating to the 1840s has been lost.

STREET NAMES

Main Street as the principal street in urban centres is an Americanism. The English equivalent would be "High Street". In the suburbs the current preference is for **Avenue, Boulevard, Circle, Court, Crescent, Drive, Heights, Lane, Place** or **Terrace** when "streets" are added as part of a subdivision. These names emphasize the supposed prestigious quality of the development. Incongruities arise when "avenues" are not tree lined; a "boulevard" should be broad, tree lined and landscaped; a "court" should be short, walled by buildings on three sides; and a "place" is a square defined by buildings.

Long streets across a town provide "landmarks of progression" that punctuate travel across the urban scene. A route north from downtown St. Catharines passes **Welland, Carlton, Scott, Linwell** and **Lakeshore,** and an east-west journey might cross **Ontario, Lake, Geneva, Vine, Niagara, Grantham** and **Bunting.** In Niagara Falls **Kalar,**

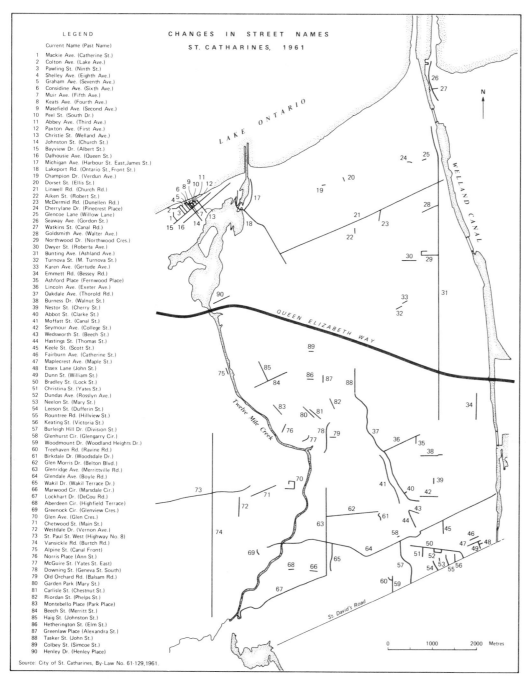

Fig. 9.1

Montrose, Dorchester, Drummond, Stanley and Victoria may be traversed successively along Thorold Stone, Lundy's and McLeod roads. These are the streets which citizens use to structure their mental maps of the city. They are the well-known routes of travel across the urban environment, which often define the edge of urban districts.

Many roads are named after a nearby physical feature. Front Streets are frequent next to a waterbody such as the Welland Canal or a river. In Chippawa are Chippawa Creek Road, Chippawa Parkway, Lyons Creek Road and Lyons Creek Parkway. Feeder Road refers to the Welland Feeder Canal, and Canal Bank Street and Canal Road are parts of the scene in Welland. It is River Road above the gorge in Niagara Falls, and the same name is used next to the Welland River in Pelham. The Niagara River Parkway follows the Niagara River from Fort Erie to Niagara-on-the-Lake, and River Road much of its length through Niagara Falls.

Riverview Boulevard and Drive, St. Catharines, follow Twelve Mile Creek. Lakeshore Road intermittently follows Lake Ontario; earlier lengths along the bluffs have been eroded, and the modern alignment is often inland from the shoreline. Port Colborne has a Lakeshore Road. Cataract Road, Thorold, heads to DeCew Falls, and Cataract Avenue, Niagara Falls, is close to the gorge. St. Catharines has Valley and Valleyview Roads, Niagara Falls a Valley Way and Effingham a Sulphur Springs Drive after the observable yellow stains where sulphur springs ooze from the rocks.

A local building or feature often leads to the naming of an associated street. Examples include Academy, Bridge, Canal, Church, College, Lock, Mill, Park, Quarry, School, Station and Townline Streets. St. Catharines has an Oblate Street, and St. Joseph Street is after an early Roman Catholic school. Niagara Falls has Armoury and Ferry Streets. In St. Catharines Academy and Church switched names in 1856, Brewery is after Taylor and Bate brewery, and Salina recalls former salt works. In Lincoln

Cave Spring, Hillside, Mountain, Pump House, Quarry and former Power Line (now Eighth Avenue) are explicit for their depicted features. Centre Street is common, though central to what former circumstances may not now be clear.

Before roads had names, deeds frequently referred to "the road leading to...". Several street names retain this tradition. St. Catharines has Ontario and Lake Streets, which head towards Lake Ontario. Compass directions include North Street, South Drive, Eastchester and Westchester, and the cardinal points may be used as prefixes, as in Northcliff, Northdale, Northglen and Northridge.

Erie Street leads to Lake Erie in Port Colborne. Niagara Street, Queenston Road and Pelham Road are self-explanatory. Further examples include Beaverdams Road (correctly Beaver Dams) in Thorold and Niagara Falls; Chippawa Road, Port Colborne; Netherby Road, Niagara Falls; Effingham Road, Pelham; and West, Station and St. Catharines Streets in Smithville.

When small centres such as Beaver Dams, Canborough, Effingham, Netherby, Sugarloaf Hill or Windmill Point recur in street names, a reasonable presumption is that these locations were formerly of greater importance than today; for instance, Beaver Dams was an early point of convergence in the road network, Netherby had an important agricultural fair, and Sugarloaf Hill and Windmill Point were places where grain might be milled.

Roads may also signify former circumstances. Brock University faces St. David's Road and Merrittville Highway, even though the Welland Canal has long since broken the route to the village of St. Davids and Merrittville is now Welland. St. David's Road, signed St. David from Highway 406, changes to St. David Street in Thorold, a confusing sequence, and Merrittville Highway probably survives from an earlier status as the St. Catharines and Merrittsville Turnpike Road. Strangely, Merrittsville no longer has an "s". The Niagara Stone and Thorold Stone Roads draw attention to the fact that they were among the rare surfaced roads of an earlier era. Portage Road, Niagara Falls, is a

Is that Hartzel Road or Hartzell Road? The street sign and bus sign offer two different versions of the same name. The street sign is correct, but the confusion is understandable. The street is named after George Hartsell, the original settler in the area between 1798 and 1826. St. Catharines Transit says Hartzell has been used since 1980 and will be changed to one L when new route signs are installed in June.

Hartzell, not Hartzel

I read and viewed the article in The Standard Feb. 12 in which a St. Catharines Transit bus showing "Hartzell" is turning onto "Hartzel" Road as indicated on the street sign. I was surprised to read that you consider "Hartzel" correct and that this spelling is going to be adopted by the transit commission in June.

My brother Charles and I are the oldest living residents who were born and raised on "Hartzell" Road and this road holds many happy memories for us.

Jack Rountree

pronounced example of reference to an earlier function.

A continuous street in terms of direction may have obtained distinctive names for different sections of its length, thereby mentally fragmenting the reality of continuity. Examples include **Ferry Street-Lundy's Lane** and **Portage Road-Main Street** in Niagara Falls; the **Lakeview Avenue-Christie Street-Mountain Street** sequence in Grimsby; and **Hartzel Road-Merritt Street** and **St. Paul Street-Queenston Street - Queenston Road** in St. Catharines. Within Niagara-on-the-Lake, a break in the continuity of east-west names occurs at King Street: from **Front** to **Ricardo**, **Prideaux** to **Byron**, **Queen** to **Picton**, **Johnson** to **Platoff**, **Gage** to **Castlereagh**.

Reasons exist for such changes in names. At Niagara-on-the-Lake, it is the transition between surveys of different dates, and the wide intermediate street later carried railway tracks. It often means crossing a former municipal boundary or the modern city limits, as when moving from St. Catharines into Thorold streets change from **Glenridge Avenue** to **Merrittville Highway**, **Burleigh Hill** to **Collier Road**, **Bradley Street** to **John Street** and **Merritt Street** to **Ormond Street**.

BRITISH LINKS

Street names after the British royal family enjoy great popularity. **King, Queen, Prince, Princess, Regent, Duke, Victoria. Elizabeth, Philip, Charles, Alexandra, Charlotte** and **Clarence** provide examples which demonstrate the long term links of Niagara with Britain and its monarchy. As no such emphasis exists on the American side of the international boundary in either Buffalo or Niagara Falls, these patriotic names indicate the cultural divergence between the Canadian parliamentary system and the American presidential form of government. Canada evolved within the British Empire, the United States broke from this link two centuries ago, and the resultant differences of association are recalled in diverse street names.

This diversity extends into streets named after the governors, generals and other senior dignitaries of the new colony: **Brock, Carleton** (misspelled **Carlton**), **Colborne, Dorchester, Drummond, Durham, Elgin, Haldimand, Murray** and **Simcoe**. Interestingly, in St. Catharines **Duke** and **Wellington** cross each other, by accident or intent, to denote the Duke of Wellington. **Bond** and **Head** may likewise indicate Sir Francis Bond Head, Lieutenant Governor of Upper Canada from 1835 to 1838.

British links of association combine with street names such as **Coronation, Crown** and **Jubilee**. The **Imperial** subdivision near **Lancaster Avenue** has **Cardiff, Coventry, Plymouth** and **Swansea** named after English and Welsh towns.

Is it by accident or design that Bond and Head cross to form Sir Francis Bond Head?

The commemoration of British victories might also be noted. Welland recalls World War II with avenues named **Achilles, Ajax** and **Exeter,** the British light cruisers that chased the German battleship Graf Spee into Montevideo Harbour in 1939; **Bishop Road** is after Billy Bishop, the Canadian air ace of World War I. St. Catharines, recalling two world wars, has streets named after **Dunkirk, Jellicoe, Trafalgar, Tunis** and **Verdun;** there is **Winston, Churchill** and his home **Chartwell.**

PIONEER FAMILIES

When streets named after pioneer settlers are considered, British names are interwoven with groups that include those of Pennsylvanian-German and Huguenot background. In St. Catharines, streets named **Anger, Ball, Bessey, Campbell, DeCew, Disher, Haight, Hartzel** (Hartsell), **Helliwell, Holmes, Martindale, Newton, Page, Scott, Winter** and **Wynn** refer to early settlers and landowners of the area. **Gertrude,** Port Dalhousie, is probably after Gertrude Pawling, wife of a Loyalist landowner.

In Lincoln (considering only the first five letters of the alphabet) streets named after early pioneer families include **Bartlett, Bennett, Christie, Claus, Culp, Davey, Dobrindt, Durham** and **Edelheim. Valentino,** after Rudolf Valentino, the silent movie star, may suggest an Italian community or developer, as might **Via Dell Monte, Valencia** and **Capri** in St. Catharines. **Aberdeen** is perhaps after Senator William Gibson who came from Aberdeenshire, Scotland; **Robbie Burns,** Beamsville, provides another glimpse of Scotland.

In Welland, **Sauer, David** and **Harriet** are related. David Sauer, a pioneer from Germany in the 1840s, settled in Willoughby Township. One son, David, married Harriet Brearly. The streets bearing the family names were purchased or inherited from the Brearley property. A further pioneer recollection is **Fell Street,** Zenas Fell being a land surveyor, merchant and Quaker.

CONSISTENT GROUPINGS OF NAMES

As befits its historic past, Niagara-on-the-Lake offers a remarkable consistency in the commemorative names for its streets. Names in the "old survey" northwest from King Street appropriately commemorate the monarchist links of the new colony through **King, Queen, Victoria, Regent, William** and **Mary** Street. **John** could be after the king of that name or some royal relative, but perhaps Colonel John Butler is intended. **Johnson** refers to Sir William Johnson, Superintendent of Indian Affairs who led actions out of Fort Niagara during the Seven Years' War in 1759; **Gage** is for Thomas Gage, who also served during the Seven Years' War and became military governor of Montreal in 1760; **Prideaux** was the British general killed in 1759 at the siege of Fort Niagara; and **Simcoe** refers to John Graves Simcoe, the first Lieutenant Governor of Upper Canada, all leading dignitaries of the Colonial period. **Front** and **Centre** bring in locational features, and **Gate** may be in the same category.

The "new survey" northeast of King Street was laid out after the War of 1812. Its street names now reflect soldiers and statesmen prominent during the Napoleonic Wars: **Byron**, **Castlereagh**, **Collingwood**, **Nelson**, **Picton**, **Platoff** and **Wellington**. The establishment of the Niagara Harbour and Dock Company in 1831 brings in the names of its officers: **Ball**, **Delater**, **Lockhart** and **Melville**. Later additions to the south include **Pafford**, a former mayor, and **Rye** after Maria Rye who ran a home for English orphans in the old court house building. Rarely is a Canadian town so neatly divided by street names that provide a commentary on the eras during which the town developed.

Consistency in the use of particular themes is also the hallmark of certain other communities. In Merritton, tree names predominated by the 1870s. **Almond**, **Birch**, **Chestnut**, **Elm**, **Hazel**, **Hickory**, **Pine** (now **Pinecrest**) and **Walnut** have survived to this day. **Beech** (changed to **Wedsworth** in 1960), **Butternut** (now **Ker**), **Cedar**, **Cherry** (now **Nestor**), **Oak** and **Spruce** have succumbed World War II brought in **Hemlock** and **Willow**, and the 1950s **Balsam**, **Fir** and **Grove**.

Niagara Falls has pursued this collective approach in certain subdivisions. Streets owned by the Veterans Land Act Authority were named after former reeves of Stamford and township officials: **Booth**, **Green**, **Hodgson**, **Rysdale** and **Watson**. The **Solar** subdivision used galactic names for its streets: **Galaxy**, **Jupiter**, **Mars**, **Mercury**, **Neptune**, **Pluto** and **Solar**. Universities are represented by **Cambridge**, **Harvard**, **McGill**, **Oxford**, **Varsity** and **Yale**, with **Eton** (an elite English school) nearby.

Near the former Stamford racetrack are **Aintree**, **Citation**, **Epsom**, **Kentucky**, **Lexington**, **Paddock Trail**, **Preakness**, **Post** and **Woodbine**. "Wood" and "Glen" as attractive sales terminology, and associated themes, are also grouped. Close to each other are **Edenwood**, **Green Boughs**, **Grouse**, **Mount Forest**, **Pheasant**, **Ridgewood**, **Sylvan**, **Thole**, **Woodfield**, **Woodgate**, and **Woodington**. In proximity are **Glendale**, **Glendoone**, **Glengary**, **Glengowan** and **Glenwood**.

Fort Erie offers "wood" suffixes in Crystal Beach with roads named **Ashwood**, **Beechwood**, **Birchwood**, **Cherrywood**, **Eastwood**, **Elmwood**, **Hazelwood**, **Lakewood**, **Maplewood**, **Oakwood**, **Rosewood**, **Westwood** and **Willowood**. **Buffalo Heights** recalls the streets of this American city, with **Bidwell**, **Chapin**, **Delaware**, **Ferry**, **Lafayette** and **Richmond**. Another subdivision has in proximity **Ash**, **Cedar**, **Cherry**, **Hickory**, **Maple**, **Peach**, **Pine** and **Spruce**. Ideally for aesthetic variation and to provide distinction within the urban environment, each street should be planted with these tree species, an approach achieved in certain English garden cities in the early twentieth century.

Welland has a subdivision of street names associated with World War II: the cruisers noted above (pg. 76) are close to **Corvette**, **Fleet** and **Navy**. **Churchill** leads to **Victory** through **Calais**, **Commando**, **Coventry**, **Dieppe**, **Dover** and **Dunkirk**. **McArthur** and **Roosevelt** are recognized as American contributors to the success of the Allied armies.

French ethnicity is expressed by some nine streets: **Chantal**, **Dauphine** (2), **Laporte**, **La Salle**, **Laval**, **Marc**, **Tanguay** and **Vanier**. These streets were built after the recruitment of French-Canadian workers from Quebec in the late-1910s and most are post-World War II. **Marc** Boulevard and **Chantal** Court were named after the children of French construction company owner Laurent Viger, of Viger Construction Company.

LOCAL DIGNITARIES AND BUSINESSMEN

Every town has its local "hero" who helped materially to establish and promote that place. **McCormick Street**, Welland, is named after B.J. McCormick who, judged "the founder of modern Welland" for his boosting activities in the early 20th century, expanded the industrial base of Welland and Crowland. He became Welland's first Industrial Commissioner, and coined the slogan "Watch Welland Grow". Chippawa has **Macklem Street** and **Cummington**

Square. The former pioneer carried on an extensive milling and distillery business in the 1790s; he owned steamboats, foundries and the Niagara to Chippawa stage coach route. James Cumming, a prominent merchant, sat in the parliament of United Canada, and was the first Warden of the new county of Welland.

Gibson Street in Beamsville is named after William Gibson, called to the Senate in 1902. He operated extensive limestone quarries at Beamsville. **Deverardo Drive** in Fonthill, refers to Dexter D'Everardo; born in Paris in 1814, he became Registrar of Deeds and the Surrogate Court, and was the first appointee to Welland County.

Prominent local people of Port Colborne honoured by street names include L.G. **Carter,** a merchant and chief contributor to the Baptist Church; George **Christmas** and A.D. **Cross,** reeves of the village; **Louis** Kinnear, a lawyer; and Thomas **Park** a collector of customs. **Fuller Crescent** in Thorold is named after Thomas Brock **Fuller,** first Anglican Bishop of Niagara, 1875, and former Rector of Thorold.

Manufacturers are represented in St. Catharines by streets such as **Frank,** after Frank Stinson who owned a distillery; **Abbey,** after a ship builder at Port Dalhousie; **McCordick,** who owned a tannery; **Adams** and **Thomas** for Thomas Adams, **Norris, Phelps** and **Woodruff,** for mill owners; and **Riordan,** for the owner of a paper mill. **Bunting** is possibly named after Thomas Bunting, a leather dealer and tanner.

St. Catharines also has streets named after former mayors: **Currie** (J.G., 1869-70); **Marren** (Patrick, 1871); **Oille** (Lucius S., 1878); **Carlisle** (Henry, 1879-81); **Rykert** (J.C., 1895-96); **Keating** (M.Y., 1899-1900); **Marquis** (A.W., 1905); **Campbell** (J.S., 1908-09); **Petrie** (James D., 1914-1915); **Lockhart** (N.J.M., 1935), **Westwood** (W.J., 1936), **Wright** (John D., 1928-29, 1937-38); **Daley** (Charles, 1939-43); **Franklin** (A.C. John, 1952-53); and **Buchanan** (Ivan D., 1961-64).

Elsewhere in St. Catharines, **Anderson** may be named after Dr. Terence W. Anderson, and **Swan** after Dr. L.C.

The Riordan Paper Mills 1898

Swan, a veterinarian. **Dwyer** is possibly after Gerald D. Dwyer, an inspector for the Separate School Board connected with St. Alfred's School and Church, and **McNicholl** and **Schwalm** after pastors at this church. **James** refers to James B. Clendennan, whose father owned most of the land from the Welland Canal to Church Street. **St. Paul Street** refers to a tavern owner at the St. Paul-Ontario Street junction, Paul Shipman.

Court and **Geneva** were named by Oliver Phelps, a major contractor for the First Welland Canal and a founder of the Hydraulic Company, the former as the intended location of the Court house when it moved from Niagara, and the latter perhaps after this town in New York State as Phelps came from that state.

Samuel Moffat, a policeman, tax collector, assessor, dog catcher, weed inspector and truant officer at Merritton from 1905 to 1915 is remembered by **Moffat Street,** and **Wilkes** recalls Arthur A. Wilkes, an assessor for Grantham Township. **Keating** was a dealer in books and stationery, and **McGuire** a dealer in wines and spirits.

LANDOWNERS AND LAND DEVELOPERS

Developers have a propensity to name roads after their family members. In Lincoln **Barry, Douglas** and **George** Streets were created, naming the sons of Herman G. Humphrey when his property was divided. On the estate of Ernest O. Drake are **Drake, Cameron** (son), **Dufferin** (Cameron's second name), **Margarette** (daughter) and **Robert** (grandson). **Jackson** is after Alvin Jackson, developer, and **Marlin** is manufactured from **Mar**(vin) and **Lin**(da), the children of Bernard Epp, a builder and subdivider at Vineland.

At Port Colborne, commemorative names resulting from the subdivision process include Mary **Fielden**, wife of the property owner; John **McRae**, owner of the subdivision; and L.G. **Stanley**, who subdivided this section. The **Steele** estate contributed **Forest** and **Clare**, daughters of C.E. Steele and **Omer**, brother, when the estate was subdivided. The development of the J.D. Thompson estate brings in James **Mitchell**, Adam A. **Davis** and William **Bell**, executors of the estate; James **Kinnear** who advised the executors; and Edmund **DeCew**, their land surveyor; **Isabel** is the daughter of L.M. Turnbull, the subdivision owner.

In St. Catharines **Harcove, Lawrence, Nello** and **Youngblut** are contractors who helped develop these respective streets. **Belton, Masterson** and **Scott** are after landowners Peter Belton, Russell Masterson and H.E. Scott. **Burleigh** is named after the family who owned land on the Niagara Escarpment where this road was cut.

INFREQUENT NAMES AND NUMBERED STREETS

In St. Catharines, **Lochinvar** was named after a special cow, and **Strathmore and Sovereign** after bulls. **Vine** may indicate not former grape growing activity, but the Vine family. **Melba** may refer to the Australian soprano opera singer, Dame Nellie Melba, or to the peach. **Export Avenue** was in the hope that industrial exports would result from this industrial subdivision.

Niagara Falls recalls the failed **City of the Falls** project, a large residential city planned in 1832 by an influential group of businessmen. They are recalled by the street names in its anticipated location: **Allan, Buchanan, Clark, Dixon, Dunn, Murray, Robinson** and **Stanley.** Streets recalling American presidents are rare, but Niagara Falls, St. Catharines and Welland have **Kennedy** and **Roosevelt Streets.** In Niagara Falls, **Stanley** is after Hon. E.G. Stanley, Secretary of the Colonial Office, **Buttrey** is named after the builder of a famous elevator across the gorge, and **Willo-Dell** for the road and golf course sounds as if fairies are to be seen, but probably refers to a former grove of willow trees and the Dell family of Scottish Presbyterians.

At Bridgeburg, now Fort Erie, streets commemorate Adam **Crook,** the first Minister of Education for Ontario, and W.R. **Phipps,** first clerk of the Forestry Department of Ontario. Streets also honour Charles N. **Glenny,** a Chairman of the School Board; Henry **Emerick,** a postmaster and first village clerk; and George **Lewis,** a postmaster and express agent.

Streets numbered after lots and concessions occur in former Niagara Township, where the north-south roads are numbered **Concession 1, 2, 3, etc.,** and their east-west counterparts are **Line 1, 2, 3, etc.** In former Louth Township, **Streets** are numbered north-south and **Avenues** east-west. The former western township line (now **Victoria Avenue,** Vineland), stands out not only for its jogged intersections where adjacent townships did not fit together, but also in terms of the contrasting approach to the naming of its discontinuous east-west cross streets; for example, **1st Avenue** becomes **Green Lane** and **2nd Avenue** becomes **John Street.** Numbered designations may also be written; for example, **3rd Street Louth** may appear as **Third Street Louth.** Fourth Avenue, known as **Middle Road** presumably because of its location between Lake Ontario and Highway 81, is also **Regional Road 77.**

Numbered streets are also to be found in South Grimsby,

where the town initials introduce a sequence with a few omissions from **SG2** to **SG21**. **First** to **Seventh Streets,** Welland, are in part occupied by the benevolent housing provision of Plymouth Cordage, an enlightened company project of the early twentieth century which provided quality living space in an open setting for its workers. Caistor has numbered **Concession Roads.**

At Wainfleet, a street labelled **19M9** is so coded for Fire Department purposes. Firelanes, which generally run between Lakeshore Road and Lake Ontario, are mostly private rights-of-way that date back to the 1950s when cottagers bought building lots from farmers along the lakeshore. Constructed across farmers' fields, they are generally numbered rather than named (e.g. **Firelane 6**) to facilitate recognition for firefighting purposes.

IN ANTICIPATION OF NEW NAMES

Thorold has prepared a list of notable persons deemed suitable for commemoration in street names. Some of the people honoured include John **Brown,** Thorold's only settler when the township was surveyed in 1788 and later a contractor for the Welland Canal, George **Couke** on whose land the formal surrender of the Battle of Beaver Dams was signed, David **Damude** and Isaac **Haney** who helped survey Thorold Township in 1788, and Rev. Daniel Ward **Eastman,** a Presbyterian minister.

Other possibilities include Israel **Swayze,** founder of Beaver Dams; the **Turney** family who owned the land where Brock University now stands; the **Singer** family, once commemorated in Singers Corners; Francis Gore **Willson** who subdivided Beaver Dams about 1914 when its vicinity and the old village were flooded for hydro-electric works; and, as one of the city's more famous sons, Sir Edward Wentworth **Beatty,** a president of the Canadian Pacific Railway who called his private car "The Thorold". An array of officials, mayors, elected members and citizens who have contributed to local endeavours are also on the list. The range of occupations and services is considerable, but more possibilities might be added to recognize the city's industrial past, its passing vessels on the Welland Canal, and to appreciate the city's ethnic structure through the receipt of worthy names from the various clubs.

The importance of such lists is that names have a serious meaning; their bestowal is an act that requires careful thought. As with all names that exist in every locality, once assigned, recorded on maps and placed in general usage, there is then the opportunity for residents, and especially school groups, to learn about the roots of their area and to use this detail to inspire an interest in the emergence and character of local environments.

Some peculiar decisions have arisen in this process of bestowal. Almost forgotten is **Alexander Muir,** whose dry dock and shipbuilding activities in Port Dalhousie were famous throughout the Great Lakes in the nineteenth century. The street named in his honour is not close to his original site and, when an opportunity came to name a small park in the area of his former dry dock, this became **Rennie Park** after another candidate.

Fort Erie has not recognized **Colonel Sir Casimir Stanislaus Gzowski,** responsible for the International Bridge spanning the Niagara River; nor is he recognized at Niagara Falls as the first Chairman of the Niagara Parks Commission. Nor is the important work of beautification by **Thomas B. McQuesten,** a later Chairman, recognized, though he established the Niagara Parks Commission School of Horticulture, spearheaded the restoration of Forts George and Erie, and introduced much of the impressive stone and iron work that bounds the river precincts at Niagara Falls.

Nor is there a street named after Mrs. **Clementina Fessenden,** largely responsible through her work in the I.O.D.E. for the establishment of Empire Day on Queen Victoria's birthday. The naming of streets, more than at the whim of a developer or official, should be the outcome of a concerted community decision-making process.

10.
The
Expanding
City

Especially since World War II in conjunction with large-scale immigration and the freedom of movement introduced by the automobile, settlements at Niagara have expanded outwards and dispersed over the adjacent countryside. Elements from the past have been used or retained, and new names have been added to the landscape through these processes of achievement.

URBAN PROMOTION

Expansion is welcomed and promoted by most municipalities. A larger population, a broader economic base and increased revenues are encouraged through boosterism, which in turn adds new phrases and slogans to the array of place names. **St. Kitts** as a longstanding abbreviation for St. Catharines, and **Port** meaning Port Dalhousie, carry a pleasant and familiar ring. So does **Garden City** for St. Catharines, which ties in nicely with **The Garden of Canada,** an earlier term for the area now generally known as the **Niagara Fruit Belt.** This resource, is also recognized at Grimsby where the town's Latin motto of "Floream Grimsby In Medio Horti" means that Grimsby flourishes in the middle of the garden.

At St. Catharines, **Garden City** evolved because of the gardens, orchards and nurseries within and around St. Catharines. It adds what should be the pleasing qualities of openness and greenery to the perceived character of this town. The name is also popular, being used by some thirty businesses and activities, including **Garden City Productions,** a theatre group. Though it sounds as if a gardener was involved, it is fortuitous that Mr. Edward Gardiner, a surveyor, had the foresight to plant the roadside trees that grace Russell Avenue and Geneva Street. It is fitting that **Gardiner Place** is named after him.

Disturbingly, the crude "We've got it all, St. Catharines", is used by the City's Chamber of Commerce, and a slogan composed of avaricious fifty dollar bills introduced "The Best Blooming Town in Ontario" in 1983. Why not focus persistently and continously on one theme, and use the traditional and welcome **Garden City** and its saintly prefix in a variety of suitable forms to advance the city?

Welland's motto "Where Rails and Water Meet" aptly reflects enthusiasm for its rail, river and canal facilities, and their strong contributions to urban evolution. Equally as pleasurable is Welland as "Rose City". A competition in 1921 among local school children selected the rose as Welland's civic flower. As the City then resolved: "We ask that it be used as freely as possible in our civic floral beds and displays and recommend its use by our citizens in their flower gardens." It is interesting that Windsor sought the same title in 1967, but relinquished this request against

Welland's prior claims.

At Thorold, **The Mountain Town** aptly refers to the city's location at the edge of the Niagara Escarpment. The slogan "Where The Ships Climb The Mountain" suitably denotes crossing the barrier of the Niagara Escarpment by successive generations of vessels on the Welland Canal.

The emblem for Port Colborne, a sailing ship within a helmsman's wheel above the slogan "The Gate of Navigation", is also apt, given the location and enterprise of this city at the southern entrance to the Welland Canal. "Power of Pride" and "Where business and lifestyle are a perfect match!" are also used by this city.

The crest for Niagara Falls, centred on the Horseshoe Falls, appropriately uses an electric generator symbolizing power and a beaver suggesting Canada. The slogan "Niagara Falls, The World's Most Famous Address" was introduced by Mayor Franklin J. Miller in the late 1950s or early-1960s. Though not officially adopted, it is used in a number of ways to promote the municipality, as is "Honeymoon Capital of the World" and "More Than Just The Falls". The former led to the ambiguous dictum by Oscar Wilde that Niagara Falls must be the second major disappointment of American married life, a witticism not appreciated by either the city fathers or tourist groups who promote the Honeymoon Capital title.

Fort Erie focuses on its distinction as the largest port of entry from the United States into Canada. "The Gateway To Canada" is used by the Chamber of Commerce, and its letterhead has a diagram of "The Friendly Circle" which incorporates both sides of the Niagara River. "Your Best Bet" is also used, capitalizing on the Fort Erie race track, but also implying that Greater Fort Erie is "the best bet" for industrial location as well as for the tourist and visitor to have a memorable time. "The Logical Place", with its obvious reference, is used by the Economic Development Department in their pursuit of industrial development for the community.

URBAN EXPANSION

As villages and towns expand in size, change their administrative boundaries or develop new activities, their traditional names may express a different character than

CITY OF PORT COLBORNE

formerly and refer to a different area. This comment applies especially to the larger centres such as Niagara Falls, Fort Erie and Grimsby. It also reflects the reduction in the number of municipalities and the more extensive areas that were alloted when a new structure of government was established with municipal reorganization in 1970.

In the case of **St. Catharines**, the name originated in Grantham Township where Twelve Mile Creek was crossed by the Queenston-Grimsby Road. Here Robert Hamilton, a merchant of Queenston, about 1780 established a store-house served by boats from the creek. Mills followed, then a church in 1796, a tavern about 1797 and a school about 1799. The tavern, later owned by Paul Shipman, gave rise to **Shipman's Corners** as the name for the new settlement.

Boosted by the Welland Canal, the **Village of St. Catharines** was incorporated as the **Town of St. Catharines** in 1845. The town's limits were extended north from Welland Avenue to Carlton Street and west of the canal in 1854. Additions at Western Hill and east from Vine Street to Grantham Avenue, followed in 1876. As a city its area expanded south to the now **Canadian National** railway tracks in 1946, and to Lockhart Drive and east to the Welland Canal in 1948.

In 1961, St. Catharines took over the **Towns of Merritton** and **Port Dalhousie,** both of which had also expanded from their original nuclei. **Grantham Township,** dissolved at the same time, also became part of the expanding city. Other settlements incorporated into the expanding matrix include **Reynoldsville, Homer, Port Weller** and **Power Glen.** When regional government was formulated, St. Catharines again expanded, this time taking over parts of **Louth Township.** Though the name St. Catharines has been used continuously since the early 1800s, its meaning and territorial extent have changed remarkably during its transition from a pioneer village to a modern city.

Many more community names exist than municipalities. These traditional and local names remain more popular and are used more frequently than the name of the administrative parent community. People tend to state that they live in **Merritton,** the **West End** or **Port Dalhousie** rather than St. Catharines; **Fonthill** or **Fenwick** rather than Pelham; **Beamsville, Vineland** or **Jordan** rather than Lincoln; **Queenston** or **Virgil** rather than Niagara-on-the-Lake; and **Crystal Beach, Ridgeway** or **Stevensville** rather than Fort Erie. Over the years, the local names have become accepted and people express a loyalty to the old, the traditional and the accustomed. As the municipalities have been awarded over-extended administrative boundaries to serve the purpose of local government, they are really "area names" that submerge local names or cause their oblivion.

An incident in 1988 indicates how conflict might arise. A water tower had been constructed in **Virgil** and the Virgil Businessmen's Association asked that Virgil be painted on the tower. Not so, decreed the Region's Public Works Department; this is the Town of Niagara-on-the-Lake and that name should be used. Virgil, however, is as an important village with a distinctive name. Road signs refer to Virgil when entering the village. Localism should have a role to play for purposes of identification in the regional vocabulary.

COMMUNITY NAMES

The **Bell Telephone Directory**, 1988, lists 128 "communities or localities" (Fig. 10.1), and more names exist within the urban areas. It is possible to live within a particular town, have a postal address in another community, and be in the telephone area of yet another place. For example, **Port Robinson** is part of Thorold; some of its telephone subscribers are listed under Port Robinson, and others under Welland and Niagara Falls, but none is listed under Thorold! Modern life is conducted in several named places.

Within the towns, when places are small, reference to a part of the town is commonly by street names, direction or in conjunction with some particular feature as in **Grimsby, North Grimsby** and **Grimsby Beach**, or **West Main Street** and **East Main Street**, Welland. With growth, new circumstances are introduced and an intermediate level of reference becomes necessary between the street and the name for the town. Several possibilities now exist, such as the ward structure, school districts or the names of new subdivisions. Every municipality contains many of these "community", "neighbourhood" and "district" names, often using the names of formerly independent centres to fulfill this important purpose.

Communities and neighbourhoods in St. Catharines identified by the City Planning Department (Fig. 10.2) include **Port Dalhousie, Grantham,** the revival of **Shipman** from Shipman Corner, **Merritton, Pelham, Louth Rural Area** and **Ryderville** (after a pioneer family) to provide the reminder of places annexed as the city expanded. **Glenridge** combines the Scottish "glen" with "edge" as a euphemism for the Niagara Escarpment, to produce a manufactured, euphonious name for suburban expansion.

Other city neighbourhoods are named after main thoroughfares (**Facer, Glendale, Haig, Linwell, Martindale** and **Oakdale**), or particular land uses (Brock **University,** Burgoyne **Woods,** Fairview **Mall,** Kernahan **Park** and **School,** Montebello **Park** and **Power** Glen). Industrial parks provide the basis for further names (**Bunting, Glendale, Louth** and **Port Weller**). **Henley** is after the regatta, and associated with Lake Ontario are **Lakeside, Lakeport** and **Lakeshore.** Distinction and character are lost when **Louth Rural Area,** a legitimate community name, is divided into neighbourhoods numbered from 1 to 6. Specific and recognized local names after landowners of long-standing would seem preferable.

In Fort Erie the wards are numbered **1, 2, 3.** In St. Catharines the numbered wards also have names: **1** is **Merritton; 2, St. Andrew's; 3, St. George's; 4, St. Patrick's; 5, Grantham** and **6, Port Dalhousie. Merritton, Grantham** and **Port Dalhousie** are former independent centres absorbed by the expanding city. The saints, the patron saints of **Scotland, England** and **Ireland,** respectively, are often written without the requisit apostrophe.

Of the "district" names in Thorold, **Thorold Centre** refers to the initiating urban nucleus. Named by compass direction from the centre are **Thorold South, North East, South East** and **South West.** External districts incorporated into the administrative bounds of the city are **Port Robinson, Blackhorse-Allanburg, Short Hills, Lake Gibson** and **Beaver Dams.** Districts of recent development are **Confederation Heights,** a residential neighbourhood, and **Brock** dignified by its university and industrial park.

Niagara Falls is divided into eight "planning communities". Five with a frontage along the Niagara River have established names: **Chippawa, Drummond, Elgin, Stamford** and **Willoughby. Crowland** is also a township name of long standing. **Northwest** is accurate in terms of direction but lacks an in-depth meaning. **Westland,** another coined name, also lacks interest.

SUBDIVISIONS

In Fort Erie **Douglastown** was developed in the mid-1950s by A.C. Douglas, and **Buffalo Heights** suggests the proximity of this American city and perhaps the origin of

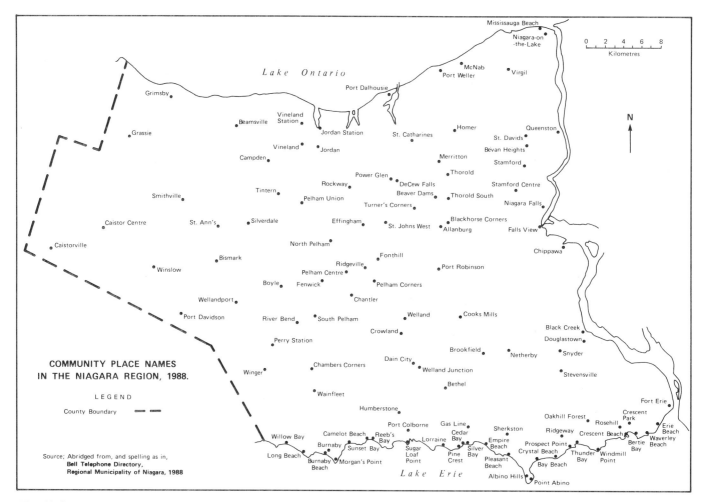

COMMUNITY PLACE NAMES
IN THE NIAGARA REGION, 1988.

LEGEND

County Boundary   ▬ ▬ ▬

Source; Abridged from, and spelling as in,
Bell Telephone Directory,
Regional Municipality of Niagara, 1988

Fig. 10.1

84

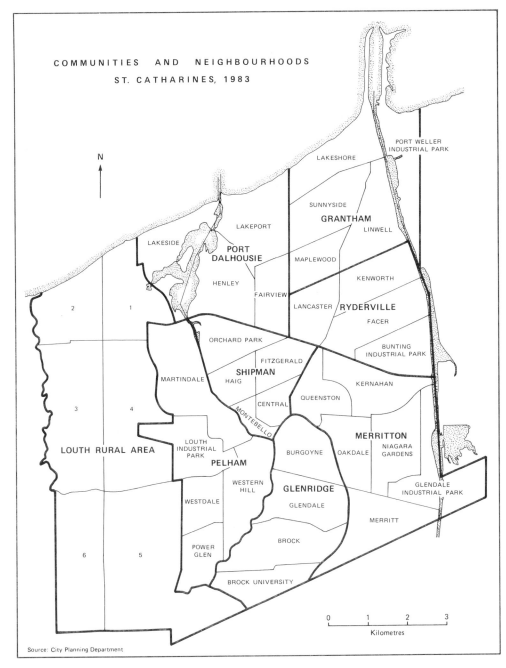

COMMUNITIES AND NEIGHBOURHOODS
ST. CATHARINES, 1983

N

PORT WELLER
INDUSTRIAL PARK

LAKESHORE

SUNNYSIDE

GRANTHAM

LINWELL

LAKEPORT

LAKESIDE

PORT
DALHOUSIE

MAPLEWOOD

KENWORTH

HENLEY

FAIRVIEW

2   1

LANCASTER   RYDERVILLE

FACER

ORCHARD PARK

BUNTING
INDUSTRIAL PARK

FITZGERALD

SHIPMAN

MARTINDALE   HAIG

KERNAHAN

3   4

CENTRAL   QUEENSTON

MONTEBELLO

MERRITTON

LOUTH
INDUSTRIAL
PARK

BURGOYNE   OAKDALE   NIAGARA
GARDENS

LOUTH RURAL AREA

PELHAM

WESTERN
HILL

GLENRIDGE

GLENDALE
INDUSTRIAL PARK

WESTDALE

GLENDALE

MERRITT

6   5

POWER
GLEN

BROCK

BROCK UNIVERSITY

0   1   2   3
Kilometres

Source: City Planning Department

Fig. 10.2

85

some of its summer residents. Subdivisions named **Crescent Beach, Bay Beach, Bertie Bay, Camelot Beach, Erie Beach, Thunder Bay** and **Wavecrest** reflect the nearby presence of Lake Erie and its sandy beaches. **Edgewood Park** is located on the edge of a wooded area, as are **Oakhill, Forest** and **Ridgewood.**

At Niagara Falls, **Cherrywood Acres** was a cherry orchard before development; the name is also used for a school and a park in this community. **Corwin Crescent** is named after a United Empire Loyalist Family who settled in Stamford Township. **Drummond Heights** is after the road named for General Sir Gordon Drummond, British commander at the Battle of Lundy's Lane. **Orchard Park,** in recognition of former fruit cultivation, has also given its name to a school. **Queensway Gardens** takes its name from the nearby Queen Elizabeth Way. **Royal** is associated with Royal Park, and **Scott** with the family farm on which the subdivision is located.

Residential developments or their streets frequently use euphonious and evocative names for purposes of prestige and to help sell their product. **Castlemere** and **Castlewood** are grandiose expressions, a castle being a fortified place of refuge but inferring also that a man's castle is his home. **Glendale** and **Glenridge**, St. Catharines, combine two pleasing words. Further examples include **Mountainview** and **Rolling Acres;** names involving a tree (**Elmwood, Oakridge, Pinecrest**) or a shrub (**Rosedale, Jasmin Crescent**), and names from nature including a wood (**Sherwood, Secord Woods**), forest (**Forest Hill**) and **Green** as a colour. Clearing orchards or vineyards and replacing them with subdivisions named **Orchard** or **Champagne Heights** provides only a nostalgic memory when houses and roads dominate the scene.

11.
Household Names

Household names are those commonly used by people who live and travel in the Peninsula. They refer to industries, where people shop or go to school, and to hospitals, shopping centres, churches and social organizations. They are the names of accustomed usage, which vary in their importance according to our ethnicity, religion and social activities, and on the basis of where we live, work and how we conduct our lives.

INDUSTRIAL AND BUSINESS ACTIVITIES

Company names are often familiar as household words and as points of identification. **General Motors** and **Thompson TRW** are important in St. Catharines; the latter incorporates Thompson the founder, and scientists **R**aymo and **W**oolridge into the TRW acronym. **Quebec and Ontario Paper** (previouly **Ontario Paper**), **Fraser** and **Hayes-Dana** are well known in Thorold; **Atlas Steel, John Deere, Union Carbide** and **Wabasso** in Welland; and **INCO (International Nickel Company)** and **Robin Hood Mills** in Port Colborne. **Nabisco** and **Cyanamid** provide industrial examples from Niagara Falls. These industrial names occasionally extend outwards to colour the personality of a given place as in the phrase "St. Catharines is a General Motors town". Hamilton as "Steel City" or Thorold as "Paper Town" provide further examples.

The wine industry is imbued with a special cachet in its names. Many companies (**Andrés, Barnes, Brights, Konzelmann, Paul Masson** and **Reif**) are named after individuals. "Château", with its suggestion of wine produced in the grounds of a French castle or manor house, is the prefix for **Château des Charmes** and **Château-Gai.** "Cellars" supposedly take us underground with **Cave Springs, Jordan and Ste-Michelle, Montravin** and **Stoney Creek.** "Estates" is used as a suffix by **Hillebrand** (previously **Newark**), **Konzelmann, Vineland** and **Willowbank. Montravin** means "vines growing on the slope of the Mountain", with mountain being a reminder of the popular term for the Niagara Escarpment.

Inniskillin, the first of the cottage wineries, was named after the farm on the Niagara Parkway where this company established. It in turn refers to Colonel Cooper of the Enniskillin (Inniskillen) regiment, who served in North America during the War of 1812 and was granted this land upon completion of his military service. **Cave Springs** is after this physical feature at the base of the Niagara Escarpment.

Steamship companies with offices in Port Colborne include **Algoma Central Railway** and **Paterson,** and in St. Catharines **Canada Steamship Lines, Misener Holdings** and **ULS International.** The **St. Lawrence**

Ontario Paper's new name Quebec and Ontario Paper

As of Sept. 1, Ontario Paper Company Ltd., which has been a household name in the Niagara peninsula for almost 75 years, under two names: Ontario Paper Company and La Compagnie de Papier Q.N.S Limitee (formerly Quebec North Shore ingual company.

A name change has been under consideration by company management for almost a year

---

Seaway Authority, the **Great Lakes Pilotage Authority** and the **Seafarers' International Union** have homes in St. Catharines. **Port Weller Dry Docks** are located in the same city. **Mrsh Engineering, Dwor Metal** and **Marine Salvage** are in Port Colborne.

Though the list of named companies is incomplete, sufficient has been written to demonstrate that Niagara has an important manufacturing base to sustain its economic activities. The named companies, whether large or small employers of labour, are an integral part of the warp and weft of life in the Peninsula.

A few manufacturing companies have given their names to nearby streets: the former International Nickel Company to **Nickel Street,** Port Colborne; the **Norton** plant to **Norton Street,** Chippawa; **Plymouth Cordage** to **Plymouth Road,** Welland; and **Pilkington Street** in Thorold South is after the former **Pilkington Glass Works.**

But many important industrial names are not remembered in the named landscape. Why is there no **McKinnon Street** in St. Catharines? Other omissions include **Packard Electric** and the **REO** automobile, **Shawinigan Chemicals, Independent Rubber** and **Carbide Willson** in St.

Catharines; **Lybster** in Merritton; **Maple Leaf Rubber** (now **Lincoln Fabrics**) in Port Dalhousie; **Algoma Steel** in Port Colborne; and **Atlas Steel, Union Carbide** and **Wabasso** in Welland. Industry, though an important basis of community endeavour, has not always been lauded when new names are created. Industrial leaders, their products and the many inventions achieved at Niagara could find greater recognition through the naming process.

COMMERCIAL NAMES

The largest shopping centres have area-wide titles. The **Pen Centre,** St. Catharines, abbreviates Niagara Peninsula and is not the American "Penn" for Pennsylvania. **Niagara Square,** Niagara Falls, contains the suggestion of serving the extent of Niagara in its name. Denoting a smaller tributary area are **Grantham Plaza, Lincoln Mall** and **Lincoln Plaza,** St. Catharines; and **Port Colborne Mall,** Port Colborne. **Scottvine Shopping Centre,** St. Catharines, is at this road junction. **Seaway Mall,** Welland, is after the nearby Welland Canal. **Fairview Mall,** St. Catharines, is both euphonious and part of the corporate name Fairview-Cadillac.

Many commercial establishments are branch operations that carry names which are provincial, national or international. The regional landscape is homogenized by such practices, that include banks, insurance companies, department stores, gas stations, supermarkets and a host of specialized retail outlets. Sameness prevails whether in Port Colborne or St. Catharines, or as between·the Niagara Peninsula and the western provinces. Whether in a mall or plaza, individuals and local identity have been lost as mass products and services have advanced.

CHURCHES AND CLUBS

With Niagara often described as a **WASP** (White Anglo-Saxon protestant) community in its early days because of its Loyalist immigration to a British colony, the saint names of its Anglican churches are reminiscent of English parishes. Four churches in the Niagara Region are dedicated to **St. John,** three to **All Saints, Christ** and **Holy Trinity,** two to **St. James,** and one to each of **Saints Alban, Barnabas, Brendan, Columba, David, George, Martin, Paul, Saviour, Stephen** and **Thomas.**

Good Shepherd, Grace and **Transfiguration** might be added, with **St. Andrew** (3), **St. Giles** and **Knox** (2) for the Presbyterian Churches, and **St. Andrew** (2) and **Trinity** for the United Church. **St. Andrew's Church,** Grimsby, may be as much after its promoter Andrew Pettit, Clerk of Grimsby Township Council, as one of the twelve apostles. Presbyterian and United churches may be named after their location, for example **Stamford Presbyterian Church,** Niagara Falls and **St. Paul Street United Church,** St. Catharines. **Mountainview United Church** perpetuates a traditional name for the Niagara Escarpment.

Churches of the Roman Catholic faith, including Ukrainian Catholic, take on a different spectrum of names. **St. Ann, St. George, Immaculée Conception, St. Mary,** **Holy Rosary** and **Our Lady** (5) now take precedence. Further saints include **Alexander, Alfred, Augustine, Catherine, Cyril** and **Methodius, Denis, Elizabeth, Helen, Kevin, Jean-de-Brébeuf, John Bosco, Joseph, Michael, Patrick, Sophia, Teresa, Thomas Aquinas** and **Vincent De Paul.** There are an **Eglise Sacré-Coeur, Star Of The Sea** churches and **St. Thomas Moore** and **Redemptoristine Nuns.**

This variety reflects the many cultural groups that comprise Niagara's population, and the churches of other faiths such as Armenian Apostolic, Greek Orthodox, Lutheran, Pentecostal and Mennonite would have to be added for a full presentation of religious names. The surprising figure of over fifty religious denominations are represented through the names of their churches at Niagara.

This diversity extends into social clubs. **Armenian, Celtic, Croatian, French, German, Greek, Irish, Italian, Polish** and **Ukrainian** are ethnic groups identified specifically in titles. Sometimes the name includes an association, as with **Club La Salle** or **Club Champlain** for French groups; **Club Roma, Casa Dante** and **Club Castropignano** for Italian clubs; and **Heidelberg** and **Rheingold** as an indication of German ethnicity. It is interesting that, when the Polish Alliance of Canada in 1967 purchased land next to Lake Ontario as a headquarters complex for its branches in Ontario, a French name, **Place Polonaise,** was chosen because it could be understood in each associated language: English, French and Polish.

A retirement home in Beamsville named **Nipponia Home for the Aged** has an interesting connection with removing Japanese from the west coast in World War II. Some of this group came to work on farms in the area and some stayed on. German cultural associations are expressed in **Edelheim Apartments,** Beamsville, and in the **Heidehof Home For the Aged** and **Lorelei Retirement Centre,** St. Catharines.

Hotel Dieu Hospital, St. Catharines

Niagara·On·The·Lake General Hospital

HOSPITALS

The system of public hospitals ensures that many hospitals carry the name of their municipality. The general hospitals at **Niagara-on-the-Lake, Port Colborne, St. Catharines** and the **West Lincoln Memorial Hospital,** Grimsby, are in this category. A regional context is included in the names for the **Greater Niagara General Hospital,** Niagara Falls, and the **Welland County General Hospital,** Welland. The **Hotel Dieu,** St. Catharines, indicates its Roman Catholic origin as a small maternity hospital operated by the Religious Hospitallers of St. Joseph. The earlier marine component of the **St. Catharines General and Marine Hospital** was dropped from the title in 1924.

Two hospitals are named after medical staff. The **Douglas Memorial Hospital,** Fort Erie, is after Dr. William Douglas. His medical practice included tending to the injured from railway accidents, and he bequeathed his estate to establish the hospital. The **Shaver Hospital for Chest Diseases,** St. Catharines, commemorates Dr. Cecil G. Shaver; opened in 1909, and first named the **St. Catharines Consumptive Hospital,** it became the **Sanatorium** and popularly the **San.**

Wings and wards. are frequently named to honour individuals and bequests. At the St. Catharines General Hospital, the **Norris Wing** is after Captain James Norris, a Hospital Board member then Chairman, also an M.P. and a steady patron of the hospital. The **McSloy Wing** commemorates this family, especially Hugh and James Ivan McSloy who owned the Canada Hair Cloth factory. The **Moore Wing** is after John Guernsay Moore, contractor, hotel owner and President of the Hospital Board from 1916 to 1952. The **Mills Wing,** after David B. Mills whose inventions include the spark plug, was built through funding by the Davella Mills Foundation; there is also a **Mills Room** in the St. Catharines Centennial Library and at the St. Catharines YMCA. Colonel R.W. Leonard, an engineer on the DeCew power project who amassed wealth from shares in the Cobalt silver mines, was a member of the Hospital Board member then Chairman, also a M.P. and a the **Leonard Hotel** was built by the same individual. The **Mack School of Nursing** owes its name to Dr. Theophilus Mack, one of the first to use the mineral waters of St. Catharines for medicinal purposes.

The **Niagara-on-the-Lake General Hospital** opened in 1919 as the **Niagara Cottage Hospital,** which changed to **Niagara Hospital** in 1955 and to its present title in 1976. The **Drope Wing,** opened in 1969, is after Kathleen I. G. Drope, a member of the board from 1954 to 1970 and chairperson from 1961 to 1963.

The Greater Niagara General Hospital carries an historical flavour with wings named in 1966 after **General Sir Isaac Brock, Laura Secord, Governor Simcoe, Lord Dufferin** and **Father Hennepin.** The **Simpson Paediatric Wing** recognizes that the hospital was a beneficiary from the estate of Andrew and Mary Elizabeth Simpson, and the **William T. Morris Wing** acknowledges a donation from the Wm. T. Morris Foundation in the United States.

At the Welland County General Hospital, the **Centennial Wing** is dedicated to Canada's centennial year. The **Woolcott Wing** is after a former executive director, F.H. Woolcott. The **Colbeck-Moffat Auditorium** is named after Drs. W.K.Colbeck and W.W. Moffatt in recognition of their outstanding service to the community.

EDUCATION

Schools, including former buildings now used for some new purpose, frequently have designed into their facade a name or initials that indicate a period of Ontario's educational history. **S.S.,** which replaced the earlier **School District (S.D.)** in 1850, refers to a **School Section,** that is the division of townships into the area served by one "common" or "elementary" school. The **S.S.** school, with an accompanying number, might also have an informal or "popular" name. A **Union School,** where the ratepayers of two school sections combined to build one school to serve both areas, results in **U.S.S. (Union School Section),** an acronym not to be confused with the United States!

Secondary Schools, also abbreviated to **S.S.** and sometimes confused with School Section, were previously **Grammar Schools,** a name established by an act of 1853. After

Brock University adopted the silhouette of Sir Issac Brock for its motif.

1871, an elite category of Secondary School intended as preparation for a university education, may have been named **Collegiate and Vocational Institute (CVI),** a title which indicated that it offered both academic and general (technical and commercial) programmes. As the Collegiate title lost its intention, many of these secondary schools adopted **High School** or **Secondary School** titles.

At the apex of Niagara's educational system since 1964, known popularly as **Brock** or **The School on the Hill, Brock University** commemorates General Sir Isaac Brock, killed at the Battle of Queenston Heights. The university, about five miles (8 km) west from the battle site is also located at the edge of the Niagara Escarpment. **Alphie's Trough,** the student pub, respects Alfred, General Brock's

horse. Monuments to horses are rare, but Alfred is also commemorated by a bronze statue at Queenston.

The **Arthur Schmon Tower** housing the library and administrative offices is after Arthur A. Schmon, Chairman of the Founders' Committee, reconstituted as the Board of Governors when the university opened and now its Board of Trustees. **DeCew Residence,** the student housing complex, recalls John DeCew of nearby DeCew Falls. The **Mackenzie Chown Complex** is after Mackenzie A. Chown, former Mayor of St. Catharines and Chairman of the Board of Trustees. Faculty members now deceased are recalled in the **Rosalind Blauer Centre for Child Care,** and the **Geoffrey Davies Memorial Room** on the ground floor of the main library. **Pond Inlet** is named after a ceremony held at this place on Baffin Island for three graduating students then working in the Northwest Territories.

Two institutions using the name "college" apply its meaning differently. To **Niagara College of Applied Arts and Technology,** Welland, it means the modern provincial system of higher education that includes both universities and colleges. At **Ridley College** it is the traditional status name for a private school offering specialized instruction to students, as at Eton College, England.

Names used at the campus of Niagara College are imaginative in their background associations. Indian links with the Niagara Area are presented through **Tecumseh Centre,** and French links through **Hennepin Hall** and **Voyageur Block.** The Battle of Lundy's Lane is recalled by

the **Lundy Building;** William Lyon MacKenzie who promoted the reform of government in Upper Canada by the **MacKenzie Building;** John Graves Simcoe as the first governor of Upper Canada by the **Simcoe Building;** and the man instrumental in achieving the Welland Canal by the **Merritt Building.** The **Black Walnut Building** refers to the tree which indicated good quality soil and attracted pioneer settlers to fertile localities. **Manera Court** is after Anthony S. Manera, President of the College from 1972 to 1977, and Ontario's youngest community college president.

Usually abbreviated to **Ridley, Ridley College** was at first **Bishop Ridley College of Ontario.** It is named after the scholarly Bishop of London, England, who was burned at the stake during the Reformation for his adherence to Protestantism. **Arthur Bishop, Gooderham** and **Merritt Houses** are named after former Presidents of the Corporation, now the Board of Governors.

Catholic schools are distinguished by the fact that most are named after saints. **Canadian Martyrs, Our Lady of Fatima, St. Alfred, St. Ann** and **St. Anthony** provide examples. **Denis Morris** however is named after a Pastor of St. Catherines Cathedral who then became Dean of Niagara and Monsignor; and **Michael J. Brennan** after a separate school trustee from 1873 to 1931. A Catholic High School in Welland is named **Notre Dame.**

The public schools have a varied range of names. Royalty and famous British personalities are recognized by **Edith Cavell, Prince of Wales, Prince Philip, Queen Mary, Sir Winston Churchill** and **Lady Spencer-Churchill.** Famous Canadian persons include **Carleton, Senator Gibson, Colonel John Butler, Lord Elgin, Pauline McGibbon, Governor Simcoe** and **Laura Secord.**

Some schools are named by location: **Beamsville, Burleigh Hill, Jordan, Merritton** and **St. Catharines Collegiate.** Other schools refer to an event: **Battlefield, Lincoln Centennial** and **Parliament Oak.** Some are named after early settlers, **Jacob Beam** and **Parnall,** or after a Superintendent of Schools, **E.I. McCulley.** French Canadian associations are recognized by schools named

Champlain and General Vanier by the Niagara South Board of Education.

A change in administration may result in a change of name, as when Lockview Park Secondary School, Port Colborne, was renamed Lakeshore Catholic High School in 1988 when leased to the Welland County Separate School Board. Other names considered were Concordia Catholic High School, St. Basil, St. Christopher, Bishop Tonos, St. Thomas Aquinas, Stella Maria Catholic High School and Aquinas Catholic High School. Protestant-Catholic divergence in naming practices, with only the latter emphasizing religion, provides an interesting cultural subtlety in the landscape.

Many schools have had a succession of names. One sequence is from Thorold County Grammar School, School of The Seven Elms, Thorold High School, Thorold-Linwell School, Thorold District High School, Thorold District Secondary School to Thorold Secondary School. In St. Catharines, Grantham Academy on Church Street, which dates from 1829, became the St. Catharines Collegiate Institute in 1872. When a new Collegiate Institute and Vocational School opened in 1923 on a street named Catherine, the old school was renamed the W.J. Robertson School after a master who had taught there from 1874 to 1912.

An interesting former name is Dewdrop School, Crowland, supposedly renamed in 1888 from S.S. 8, Crowland Township during repainting when a drop of dew fell into a pail of paint. Apocryphal, probably not, but certainly a fanciful and unusual name for a school that survived to the late 1950s.

When a succession of schools has developed on or close to the same site, their sequence of comparable names has often become a significant part of the public esteem for that locality. An interesting example is the St. Johns Outdoor Studies Centre, which opened in the two-room St. Johns Public School that had been used for public education from 1958 to 1968. The outdoor centre was promoted by E.C. (Ted) Brown, a local ratepayer, now

Lockview name goes

It is off with the old and on with the new for Lockview Park Secondary School in Port Colborne.

The school, owned by the Niagara South Board of Education, has been leased to the Welland County Separate School Board, and last night had its name changed to Lakeshore Catholic High School.

Trustees had eight names to choose from with the Port Colborne advisory committee favoring Concordia Catholic High School. Other names suggested were: St. Basil; St. Christopher; Bishop Tonus; St. Thomas Aquinas; Stella Maria Catholic High School and Aquinas Catholic High School.

commemorated in the school's Ted Brown Room which records the history of St. Johns.

The St. Johns Public School was located on the same site as the Saint John's Schoolhouse (note the full rendering of Saint and the apostrophe), built in 1879 as Union School Section No. 4 (U.S.S. No. 4). This building in turn succeeded the Common School, 1804 - 1844, which was restored in 1973 to contribute to programmes of the Outdoor Studies Centre; the common school was the St. John West Schoolhouse, a now defunct village name, but popularly called the Old Schoolhouse when a new building was constructed.

CJFT 530
FORT ERIE RADIO

LIBRARIES, RADIO STATIONS, THEATRES AND OPEN SPACE

Public libraries are usually named after their location, as with the **Fort Erie Public Library,** and its branches at **Crystal Beach** and **Stevensville;** a neat, coined amalgamation of two locations is **Crystal Ridge Branch. Library.** Sometimes important local names are used, as in the **Rittenhouse Branch** of the Lincoln Public Library, and the **William Hamilton Merritt Branch** of the St. Catharines Public Library.

Four-letter call signs are used to identify broadcasting stations. The first letter C denotes a Canadian broadcasting outlet, and the second letters **B, F, H, I, J,** and **K** are the Canadian broadcasting series. The varied combination of letter arrangements may carry a specific meaning. **CKTB,** St. Catharines, was named after the Taylor and Bate Brewery, but local folklore adds that the call letters refer to a **C**ool **K**eg of **T**aylor and **B**ate or that **C**anadians **K**now **T**heir **B**eer. In **CJFT,** Fort Erie, **FT** stands for the fort and Fort Communications Inc. owns the radio station.

The **Shaw Festival Theatre** opened in 1973 in Niagara-on-the-Lake. Staged initially in the Old Court House for the Niagara District, the plays of George Bernard Shaw provide the basis for the annual programme. Shows are now presented in the **Festival, Court House** and **Royal George Theatres.** The Festival itself began in the early 1960's.

Lord Dufferin, Governor General of Canada from 1872 to 1878, warmly supported the concept of a public park and open space along the river in the immediate vicinity of Niagara Falls. As the Dominion government would not get involved, the Ontario legislature in 1885 passed an Act for the Preservation of the Natural Scenery about Niagara Falls. **Cynthia** and **Clark Hill Islands,** purchased in 1886, were renamed **Dufferin Islands** after the Governor General.

They are overlooked by **Oak Hall,** the former home of Sir Harry Oakes, who was later murdered in the Bahamas. His name introduces the **Oakes Garden Theatre,** a formal garden in the Greek style at the corner of River Road and Clifton Hill which he bequeathed to the city. The Horseshoe Falls and the American Falls are the staged backdrop for these gardens.

Queen Victoria Park, after the British monarch, opened in 1888 under the auspices of the **Queen Victoria Niagara Falls Park Commission.** This cumbersome name was changed to **Niagara Parks Commission (NPC)** in 1927 to reflect that the total river frontage was now under the mandate of this provincial authority. **Charles Daley Park** on Lake Ontario, a recreational and camping park separate from the main sequence, is named after the Hon. Charles Daley, Chairman of the Commission from 1943 to 1947 and previously a mayor of St. Catharines. Of particular note for its contributions to the art of landscaping is the **Niagara Parks Commission School of Horticulture,** originally the **Training School for Apprentice Gardeners.**

Conservation areas operated by the **Niagara Peninsula**

Conservation Authority are named mostly after their key attraction: **Balls Falls, Chippawa Creek** and **Long Beach.** The name **Woodend** was selected by its previous owner, the Thomson family, from the ancestral home of the Heslop family at Woodend, Cumberland, England. Presumably by intention it also denotes where the "woods end"; to the east the wooded slopes of the Niagara Escarpment terminate at a cleft, now followed by the Queen Elizabeth Way. Interestingly, **Lake Niapenco** at Binbrook is not an Indian name as is sometimes stated, but cleverly manufactured as the outcome of a school contest from the initial letters of the agency, **Niagara Pen**insula Conservation Authority.

Private open space along the recreational shoreline of Lake Erie created a naming issue when in 1965, **Sherkston Beach, Empire Beach** and **Pleasant Beach** urged the Canadian Permanent Committee on Geographical names to add the designation of **Resort** to these names for inclusion in gazetteers and on official maps. The request was disallowed because it advertised a private enterprise facility.

Conclusion

When he was appointed in 1988 to set up a toponymy programme for the government of the North-West Territories, Randy Freeman stated: "The whole field of toponymy is very young. It used to be that the names of geographical features were just things to fill up the spaces on maps.... Now there is a marked worldwide trend to acknowledge the cultural and historic importance of names".

At Niagara, some early Indian and French accentuations exist, but the emphasis is on British names. They have been part of an ongoing tradition since the early days of pioneer settlement when the townships were named by the colonial authorities, and have remained an integral part of the Peninsula landscape through later circumstances. They include English, Welsh and Scottish surnames, names from places in Britain, and names associated with people and events connected with that nation.

Modern evidence for the longterm British influence includes **Queen Victoria** Park in Niagara Falls, the naming and opening of the **Queen Elizabeth** Way, the knightly prefix to the **Sir** Adam Beck Generating Station which is not repeated on the Robert Moses Generating Station facing across the Niagara River, and many royal, ducal and British town names for streets. The traveller to New York by rail may start his journey on Canada's **Via Rail,** a rail**way;** after crossing the Niagara River, it becomes the American **Amtrak Service,** a rail**road.**

This British pattern is overlaid by a series of other pertinent associations, especially the imprint of German settlers who arrived either through the disbanded Butler's Rangers, direct from the United States through social or religious pressures within that nation, or direct from Western Europe. Later immigrants have left a less assertive imprint on the local nomenclature, largely because it was an anglicized community and the landscape had been named before their arrival.

Because of proximity to the United States, an American influence can also be detected. This includes a few names after American presidents and business leaders, the transferred use of their terminology in expressions like **Creek, Corners, Main Street, Township** and **Pond,** and placing **River** after the named watercourse.

Certainly not all names have a personal association or connotation. Some have been invented or refer to objects to suit the circumstances of the period, and many names have been subject to change since their inception. But the total provides a rich repository of fact and speculation to help understand the character of the Niagara Peninsula as a personalized creation. Names have a meaning, the land has a history and a modern character, and it is our responsibility to pass on the best of these attributes to new generations.

Appendix I

A Classification Of Names Across Niagara

1. Names of Amerindian origin: **Niagara, Chippawa, Onondaga.**

2. Names of French origin: **Grand** River, Point **Abino, Champlain** Street.

3. Commemorative names that honour the memory and serve as memorials to important people and noted events. They may be applied at the time, or subsequently, and include:
    (i)   Distinguished British persons: Fort **George, Queen Victoria** Park, **Sir Winston Churchill** School.
    (ii) Prominent national individuals: **Senator Gibson** School, Port **Dalhousie; Merritt**on.
    (iii) Prominent local individuals: **Zimmerman** Avenue, **Burgoyne** Bridge, St. **Davids.**
    (iv) Prominent Americans: **Mather** Arch, **William B. Rankine** Generating Station, **Kennedy** street names.
    (v)   Wars and battles: **Dunkirk, Dieppe** and **Verdun** Streets.
    (vi) Distinguished events: **Centennial** Park, St. Catharines, 1967, after the Canadian centennial; and St. Catharines **Centennial** Library, 1976, after the centennial of the city.

4. Transferred names:
    (i) Names introduced by the controlling agencies of government: the townships of **Grantham, Grimsby, Wainfleet.**
    (ii) Names introduced as a reminder of former circumstances: **Palatine** Hill, **Tintern, Tennessee** Avenue.

5. Cultural names linked with selected traits of individuals or groups:
    (i)   Religious: **Jordon, Wesley** Avenue, **Quaker** Road.
    (ii) Classical: **Homer, Virgil, Ariadne.**
    (iii) Literary: **Shakespeare** Avenue, **Robbie Burns** Road, **Shelley** Avenue.
    (iv) Ethnic groups: New **Holland,** Club **Roma,** Little **Armenia.**

6. Possessive names identify a feature after a local person, family, business or industry, and are probably the largest category:
    (i)   Male Christian names: St. **Johns,** St. **Paul** Street, St. **Davids.**
    (ii)   Female Christian names: St. **Anns;** St. **Catharines,** St. **Mary's.**
    (iii) Surnames: **Smith**ville, **Usshers** Creek, **Morgans** Point.
    (iv)   Pioneer settlers and landowners: **Lundy's** Lane, **Martindale** Pond, **Beams**ville.
    (v)   Mills: **Ball's** Falls, **DeCew** Falls, **Cooks** Mills.
    (vi)   Industry: **Nickel** Beach, **Plymouth** Road, **Pilkington** Street.
    (vii) Businessmen: **Phelps** Street, **Merritt**on, **McCormick** Street.
    (viii) Canal Engineers: Port **Weller, Killaly** Street, **Keefer** Street.

The possessive category may be divided into a range of professional, service and industrial sub-categories as many different employment, ethnic and social groups are involved. Examples introduced in the text include municipal officers, industrial leaders, teachers and school officials, land developers, mayors and politicians. Pards and public buildings may be named after their benefactors, former professional staff, or the "Chairman of the Board of Govenors".

7. Descriptive names introduce the characteristic quality of a feature, expecially of physical objects:
   (i) Colour: **Black** Creek, **Green** Lane, **Tea** Creek.
   (ii) Shape: **Short** Hills, **Horseshoe** Falls, The **Whirlpool.**
   (iii) Size: **Grand** River, **Little** Rapids, The **Mountain.**
   (iv) Composition: **Gravelly** Bay, **Crystal** Beach, **Mud** Lake.
   (v) Relative location: **North** Grimsby, **Twelve Mile** Creek, **West** Landing.
   (vi) Signifying a direction: **Merrittville** Highway, **Lake** Street, **Toronto, Hamilton and Buffalo** Railway.
   (vii) Flora: **Willow** Bank, **Tamarack** Swamp, **Cranberry** Marsh.
   (viii) Fauna: **Goat** Island, **Rattlesnake** Ledge, **Beaver** Dams.
   (ix) Agriculture and horticulture: **Vineland**, **Nursery** Lane, **Cherry** Avenue.
   (x) Trees: **Almond, Birch** and **Chestnut** Streets.
   (xi) Historic features: **Portage** Road, **Thorold Stone** Road, **Electric** Park.
   (xii) Former landscapes: **Marsh**ville, **Swamp** Road, **Towpath** Road.
   (xiii) Geological terminology: Niagara **Escarpment,** Iroquois **Shoreline,** Fonthill **Kame.**
   (xiv) Climate: **Hurricane** Road, **Rainbow** Bridge, **Thunder** Bay.
   (xv) A suffix added to the end of a word for emphasis: Beams**ville,** Queens**ton,** Allan**burg.**
   (xvi) The international boundary: **Peace** Bridge, Mather **Memorial Arch, International** Bridge.
   (xvii) Municipal Status
       Obsolete: **County** of Welland, Niagara **District, Police Village** of Camden.
       Current: **Regional Municipality** of Niagara, **City** of St. Catharines, **Town** of Niagara-on-the-Lake.

8. Shift names transferred from an originating feature to a different object: Niagara **Peninsula,** Regional Municipality of **Niagara,** and City of **Niagara Falls** from the Niagara River.

9. Incident names referring to the scene of an event: **Parliament Oak School** (Niagara-on-the-Lake) where the first parliament of Upper Canada was held; the War of 1812 recalled by **Brock**'s Monument, Queenston Heights; **Hurricane** Road to an earlier swathe of devastation.

10. Manufactured names:
   (i) The use of initials or introductory letters: Lake **Niapenco, Linhaven** Home For The Aged, Thompson **TRW.**
   (ii) Epithets: **Mountain Town** (Thorold), **Garden City** (St. Catharines), **Rose City** (Welland).

(iii) Catch phrases: **Where Rails and Water Meet** (Welland), **The Gate of Navigation** (Port Colborne), **Honeymoon Capital of the World** (Niagara Falls).

(iv) Felicitous, euphonious and evocative names: **Sunnyside, Glenridge, Cherrywood Acres.**

11. Incorrect names.

(i) An error was made when the name was written: **Amigari** for Amigan; **Victoria Street,** St. Catharines, should have been Vittoria after Vittoria Shickluna and also that placename in Malta; **Carlton** for Carleton Street, St. Catharines.

(ii) An error has arisen during use: Point **Albino** for Point Abino.

(iii) Use of an abbreviation: **Canboro** for Canborough; **Gainsboro**'for Gainsborough.

12. Names from folk lore and traditional beliefs: **Maid of the Mist, Ariadne, Neptune's** Staircase.

13. Numbers used instead of names: **First** Street, Highway **20**, Lock **7.**

14. Acronyms: **QEW** for The Queen Elizabeth Way; **GM** for General Motors: **N.S. & T.** for the Niagara, St. Catharines and Toronto streetcar system.

15. Witticisms. **N.S. & T.,** "Never Starts on Time"; the **Sandfly Express** between Fort Erie and Erie beach; **CKTB** radio station, a "Cool Keg of Taylor and Bates".

16. Exaggerated names: Fort Erie, Snake Hill and **Pacific** Railroad; **The Mountain** for Niagara Escarpment; a **Boulevard** when only a two-lane road exists.

Acknowledgements

The first debt of gratitude is to Sheila M. Wilson, now retired from the St. Catharines Public Centennial Library, for providing and verifying facts, for reading and improving successive manuscripts, and for helping with the index. Her love of words and phrases comes staunchly through in many sections of this narrative.

Michael Smart, Executive Secretary of the Ontario Geographic Names Board, Toronto, and Helen Kerfoot, Acting Executive Secretary of the Canadian Permanent Committee on Geographic Names, Ottawa, have been more than helpful in providing access to their files. The former has also reviewed the final draft, and the latter initiated this work when she invited the author to contribute to **CANOMA** about names along the Niagara River. John Burtniak, Special Collections Librarian, Brock University, has provided much historical advice throughout the preparation of this book.

Librarians in the Niagara Peninsula have provided information advice from their records. Particular thanks are due to the Main Library and the Map Library at Brock University, and to reference and local history authorities in the municipal libraries. Museum curators have added their generous quota of wisdom and expertise. The Provincial and Federal Archives have assisted materially, as has Colin Duquemin of the St. John's Outdoor Studies Centre and colleagues in the Departments of History and Geography at Brock University.

These thanks of warm appreciation are extended to numerous hospitals, school boards, industries, Chambers of Commerce, and to the many departments of regional and municipal government that have been approached. The request for the meaning of a name may occasion no surprise. It also sometimes led to interest in the topic at the receiving end of a telephone call. "I have always wanted to know that", said one bemused secretary. And another remarked, "Its gibberish to me, but I shall try to find out if a reason exists." The research for this study has itself provoked interest in the topic.

The Bibliography is a selective culling of the major published sources that have been consulted. There is also a hearty appreciation for the rich data included in numerous histories by local authors, social groups, churches, businesses, clubs and ethnic-cultural organizations. Local folklore has added much pertinent detail to the above account.

The typing of successive manuscripts has been undertaken with willing enthusiasm by Colleen Catling, Secretary, Department of Geography, Brock University, and under the able guidance of Jenny Gurski in Clerical Services. The maps have been drawn by Loris Gasparotto, Cartographer in the Department of Geography, Brock University. The author gratefully acknowledges the contributions by Brock University towards this publication.

With all the above advice, there should be no errors. Those that occur are my responsibility. But let the reader be aware of the fact that, when the meaning and sometimes the spelling of names are under discussion, "correct" answers often do not exist — only possibilities, conjecture and different possible interpretations to explain the meaning of our landscape at Niagara. Nor has it proved possible to include every name that exists. There will be disappointment at the exclusion of certain family or business names, for example when streets and industrial characteristics are under discussion, but this in no way implies a lesser importance to that group.

With Sheila Wilson, I warmly thank all who have assisted so materially towards our efforts at elucidation.

October 1989

John N. Jackson
Department of Geography
Brock University.

A Select Bibliography

Armstrong, G.H. *The Origin and Meanings of Place Names in Canada.* Toronto: Macmillan, 1930.

Campbell, F.W. *Canada Post Offices 1755/1895.* Lawrence, Mass.: Quarterman, 1972.

Canadian Permanent Committee on Geographical Names. *Principles and Procedures for Geographical Naming,* 1987, and *Gazetteer of Canada: Ontario,.*4 ed. Ottawa: Department of Energy, Mines and Resources, 1988.

Carnochan, J. *History of Niagara.* London: Phelps, 1984, 2v, and *Ghost and Post Offices of Ontario.* Oakville: Personal Impressions Publishing, 1986.

Carter, F.E. *Place Names of Ontario.* Toronto: Briggs, 1914; reprinted by Mika (Belleville), 1973.

Duff, L.B. "Names Are Pegs To Hang History On", in *Ontario Historical Society, Papers and Records,* v. 23, 1926.

Ekwall, E. *The Concise Oxford Dictionary of English Place Names,* 4 ed. Oxford: Clarendon Press, 1960.

Freeman, R in Benyk, P. "Getting the names straight" in *Uphere,* July - August, 1988.

Gardiner, H. F. *Nothing But Names.* Toronto: Morang, 1899.

Gourlay, R. *Statistical Account of Upper Canada ...,* v.1.   London: Simpkin and Marshall, 1822.

Green, E. "The Niagara Portage Road" in *Ontario Historical Society, Papers and Records,* v. 23, 1926.

Hamilton, W. B. *The Macmillan Book of Canadian Place Names.* Toronto: Macmillan, 1978.

Jackson, J.N. "Names along Ontario's Niagara River Parkway" and "Names along the Welland Canals" in *CANOMA,* v. 11.2, 1985 and v. 12.2, 1986.

Jones, A. and D. Smith, "Names of the Rivers and Creeks as they are called by the Mississagues...", 1796 in *Surveyors Letters L & F.,* v. 28. Toronto: Ontario Department of Lands and Forests.

Junius (Seymour Phelps). "St. Catharines A-Z" in *St. Catharines Journal,* 1856; reprinted St. Catharines and Lincoln Historical Society, 1967.

Mika, N. and H. *Places in Ontario: Their Name Origins and History,* 3v. Belleville: Mika, 1977-1983.

Ommanney, C.S.L., Chairman, Advisory Committee on Glaciological and Alpine Nomenclature. *Glossary of Generic Terms in Canada's Geographical Names.* Ottawa: Energy, Mines and Resources, 1987.

Ontario Geographic Names Board. *Naming Ontario: A Guide to the Collection of Geographic Names.* Toronto: Ministry of Natural Resources, 1977, and *Principles of Geographic Naming.* Toronto: Queen's Printer, 1975.

Ontario Geographic Names Board. *Naming Ontario: A Guide to the Collection of Geographic Names.* Toronto: Ministry of Natural Resources, 1977, and *Principles of Geographic Naming.* Toronto: Queen's Printer, 1975.

Page, H.R. *Illustrated Historical Atlas of the Counties of Lincoln and Welland.* Toronto: H.R. Page, 1876.

Rannie, W.F. *Names in Lincoln: A Study of Street, Road and Other Names in an Ontario Town,* Lincoln: W.F Rannie, 1975.

Rayburn, A. *Geographical Names of Prince Edward Island.* Ottawa: Department of Energy, Mines and Resources, Surveys and Mapping Branch, 1973.

Rayburn, A. *Geographical Names of Renfrew County: Geography Paper 40.* Ottawa: Geographical Branch, Department of Energy, Mines and Resources, 1967.

Rydford, J. *Indian Place Names: Their Origin, Evolution and Meaning* .... Norman: University of Oklahoma Press, 1968.

Severance, F.H. *An Old Frontier of France* .... in *Buffalo Historical Society Publications,* v. 20-21. New York: Dodd, Mead, 1917.

Smart, M.B. "Niagara Peninsula Names: A Cultural Heritage" in *Immigration and Settlement in the Niagara Peninsula: Third Annual Niagara Peninsula History Conference.* St. Catharines: Brock University, 1981.

Smith, G.H. "The Street Names of Port Colborne" in *Welland County Historical Society, Papers and Records,* v.5, 1938.

Smith, W. H. *Smith's Canadian Gazetteer.* Toronto: H. and W. Rowsell, 1846.

Stewart, G.R. "A Classification of Place Names" in *Names,* v.2.1, 1954.

Tait, G. "Street and Place Names and Early Reminiscences". *Welland County Historical Society, Papers and Records,* v.3, 1927.

Taylor, C. and M. Parnell *The Mini-Atlas of Early Settlers in the District of Niagara.* St. Catharines: The Historical Society of St. Catharines, 1983.

Taylor, I. *Names and Their Histories.* London: Rivington, Percival, 1896; and Taylor, I. *Words and Places.* London: Macmillan, 1864.

Index

The chapter headings and their sub-titles indicate the themes that have been developed. The text is **not** an alphabetical arrangement of place names, but rather a discourse on the varying influences over time which have served to imprint certain names on the Niagara landscape. As selective examples have been used to illustrate the different name categories, this index serves to list the names actually mentioned in the text. All names are classified to one of six groups: Community, Engineering, Local, Physical Features, Roads and Ships.

This listing of names might also be used to indicate the reader's knowledge about the Niagara Area, and as a game. How many of the indexed names can be described and located?

1. Community Place Names

(Administrative Units, Cities, Corners, Districts, Forts, Mills, Neighbourhoods, Ports, Post Offices, Railway Stations, Subdivisions, Towns and Villages)

34; Lower Twenty 19; Loyalist Village 35; Lune(n)burg 28; Marshville 20,52; Martindale 83; McNab 64; Mecklenburg 28; Merritton 31,46,49,52,82,83; Merritt(s)ville 46,49,52; Michigan Side 58; Mississauga Beach 63; Monck County 30; Montague 61; Montebello 83; Montrose 62,64; More Than Just the Falls 81; Moulton 62; Mountain Town 81; Mountainview 86; Mount Dorchester (Township) 30,35; Moyer's Corners 42; Muir Settlement 61; Muirsport 53; Municipal Corporations, see by name; Narrows 19; Nassau 28; Netherby 61,72; New, as prefix, 43; Newark 9,35,36; New France 23; New Germany 43; New Holland 43; New Landing 34; Newman Mill 64; Niagara(-on-the-Lake) 9,25-26,31,35-36,38,82; Niagara County, N.Y. 26; Niagara District 28-29; Niagara Falls 22,26,32,36,81; Niagara Falls, The World's Most Famous Address 81; Niagara (River) Frontier 14,26; Niagara Region, see Regional Municipality of Niagara; North East (Thorold) 83; North Riding 30; Northwest (Niagara Falls) 83; Oakdale 83; Oakhill 86; Oakridge 86; Ontario 22-23,25,60; Orchard Heights 86; Orchard Park 86; Ortville 43; Osborne's Corners 40; Overholt 61; Paper Town 87; Pelham 31,34,82,83; Pelham Corners 38; Perry (Station) 61; Petersburg(h) 51; Pinecrest 86; Pleasant Beach (Resort) 95; Police Villages 32; Polling Districts 28; Port 80; Port Beverley 51; Port Colborne 51; Port Dalhousie 14,48,49,51,82,83; Port Davidson 38,51; Port Fanny 51; Port Maitland 51; Port Muir 53; Port Robinson 48,49,51,83; Port Weller 51,53,82,83; Power Glen 17,63,82,83; Power of Pride 81; Protestant Hill 52; Province of Canada 22; Quaker Township 43; Quebec 23; Queenston, and variants, 10,22,23,32,34,38,82; Queensway Gardens 86; Region 30; Regional (Municipality of) Niagara 14,26,30; Reynoldsville 63,82; Ridgeville 15,40,46; Ridgeway 15; Ridgewood 15,25,86; Ridings 28,30; Robbins 61; Rolling Acres 86; Rose City 80; Rosedale 86; Rosedene 61; Royal 86; Ryderville 83; St., as prefix 42,45; St. Andrew's Ward 83; St. Anns 42,61; St. Catharines, 19,29,32,33,38,42,45,50, 60,80,82,87; "St. Catharines is a General Motors Town" 87; St. Catherines 38,42; St. Davids (David, David's) 21,32,38,40,45,46; St. George 40; St. George's Ward 83; St. Johns 40; St. Kitts 80; St. Mary's 42,60; St. Patrick's Ward 83; Saltfleet 31,34; Saratoga of the North 62; Sault Ste Marie (Soo) 55; Scott 86; Second Riding 30; Secord Woods 35,86; Seven Mile Stake 52; Sherks(ton) and Beach (Resort) 61,95; Sherwood 86; Shipman's Corners 82,83; Short Hills 83; Shriner's 64; Silverdale 61; Singer Corner 79; Six Nations Reserve 23; Slabtown 44,52 Slater's Dock 64; Smithville 32,33,39,46,61; Snake Hill Grove 62; Snyders Mills 42; Solar 76; Solid Comfort 62; South East (Thorold) 83; South Riding 30; South West (Thorold) 83; Stamford (Green) 30,31,34,64,83,89; Steel City 87; Steeles Corners 40; Stevensville 39,46,61,82; Stonebridge 49,51; Stoney Creek 10,34; Stop 19,64; Street's Mills 40; Stromness 52; Stumptown 40 Sunday's Settlement 43; Suspension Bridge 60; Temperanceville 40,46; Ten 45; Ten Broek's Corners 38; Ten Mile Creek 45; Tennessee 62; Third Riding 30; Thorold 31,34,40,81,87; Thorold Centre 83; Thorold South 83; Thunder Bay 86; Tintern 62; Toronto 30; Town Line (Townline) 64,67,69; Township 36; Township Nos. 1,2,3 and 4 30; Turners Corners 38; Twelve 19; United States of America 28; Upper Canada 22,23; Upper Four 19,44; Upper Landing 23; Upper Settlement 34; Upper Ten 19,45; Usshers Creek 40; Victoria 60; Victoria Park 62; Vienna Hamlet 61; Ville, as suffix 45-46; Vineland (Station) 18,32,60,82; Vinemount 18; Virgil 19,38,44,82; Wainfleet 20,30,31,34,52; Watch Welland Grow 76; Waterloo 60; Wavecrest 86; Welland, County and City 30,46,49,52,80; Welland Canals Corridor 49,54; Welland Junction 49,58; Wellandport 19,51; Welland Vale 16; Wellington County 29; Wentworth County 29-30; Wesley Park Station 62; West End 82; West Landing 34; West Niagara 35; Western Hill 58; West Lincoln 34; Westport 52; We've got it all, St. Catharines 80; Where Rails and Water Meet 80; Where The Ships Climb The Mountain 81; Where business and lifestyle are a perfect match! 81; White Pigeon 10,42; Widderburn 62; Willoughby 19,30,31,34,83; Winona 10,22,25,60; Winslow 62; York 30; Your Best Bet 81.

2. Engineering Names

(Bridges and Tunnels, Canals, Hydro-electric Installations, Railways, Streetcars and Their Companies)

Abandoned Channel 47; Amtrak 96; Aqueduct 48,52; Asylum Basin 48; Big Highway Ship Canal 52; Boat Canal 52; Bridges, numbered 69; Buffalo and Lake Huron Railway 62; Buffalo, Brantford and Goderich Railway 62; Canada Air Line 58; Canadian National 39,58; Canadian Niagara Generating Station 63; Canadian Pacific 61;

Canadian Southern 61; Canal Valley 44; Cataract Power Company 63; Chambly Canal 47; Chippawa Channel Cut, and Power Canal 18,23; Clinton's Ditch 52; Coniagas Pond 48; Crazy Crotchet 52; DeCew Generating Station 17,63,90; Deep Cut 48; Electrical Development Company 64; Electric Park 64; Erie and Ontario Railway 40,62; Erie Canal 23,52; Feeder Canal 48; Fifth (Welland) Canal 49; First (Welland) Canal 47,48; Flight Locks 50; Fort Erie, Snake Hill and Pacific Railroad 62; Fourth (Welland) Canal 48; Garden City Skyway 69; Goose Island 48; Grand Trunk 58,62; Grass Island, Pool and Weir 18,64; Great Gorge Route 64; Great Western Railway, including Canada Air Line 39-40,58,60-61; Guard Lock 50; Henley Island 48; Homer Skyway 69; Hydraulic Company and Raceway 50; Hydro-Electric Power Commission of the Province of Ontario 64; International Bridge (Company) 60; International Control Dam 64; International Railway 64; Lachine Canal 47; Lake Gibson 10,63; Lake Moodie 63; Lake Niapenco 95; Lake Pattersson 63; Lewiston-Queenston Bridge 69; Lift Locks 49; Little Brook 52; Locks, numbered 1-8 50,63; Maid of the Mist Incline Railway, Landing and Pool 21; Main Street Tunnel 69; Manchester Ship Canal 47; Marlatt's Pond 48; Martindale Pond 48; McCarthy's Pond 52; Merritt Island 52; Merritt's Ditch 52; Michigan Central 58,62; Montrose Yards 62; Mud Lake 49 Neptune's Staircase 50; New Canal Swing Bridge 64; New York Central 61; Niagara Canal 47; Niagara Cantilever Bridge 26,60; Niagara Falls International Bridge Company 60; Niagara Falls Power Company 64; Niagara Falls Suspension Bridge Company 60; Niagara Mohawk Power Corporation 64; Niagara Railway Steel Arch Bridge 60; Niagara, St. Cathairnes and Toronto Railway (N.S.& T) 26,64; Niagara Suspension Bridge 26; Niagara Falls International (Suspension) Bridge Company 26,60; Old Canal 47; Old Canal Swing Bridge 64; Ontario Hydro 64; Ontario Power Company 64; Ontario Southern 63; O'Reillys Bridge 38; Paddy Miles Express 62; Peace Bridge 68; Peanut Special 62; Peg-Leg Railway 63; Plant No. 3, Niagara Falls Power Company 64; Power Glen 17; Queenston-Chippawa Power Development 64; Queenston Heights Bridge 69; Queenston-Lewiston (Suspension) Bridge 65,68; Railway Incline 48; Rainbow Bridge 19,65,68; Ramey(s) Bend 48; Robert Moses Generating Station 96; St. Lawrence Seaway Authority 47; Sandfly Express 62; Sault St. Marie (Soo) Canal 47; Second (Welland) Canal 47; Ship Canal 47-48; Shriner's Pond 48; Sir Adam Beck Generating Station 23,64,96; Slater's Dock 64; Spanish Aero Car 17; Stop 19,64; Suspension Bridge 58,60; Tête-de-Pont (battery) 27; Third (Weland) Canal 47; Thorold (railway car) 79; Thorold Tunnel 69; Toronto, Hamilton, and Buffalo (T.H. & B.) 61; Toronto Power Company 64; Tower Inn Terminal 64; Townline Tunnel 69; Upper Steel Arch Bridge 68; Via Rail 96; Welland Canal 14,47-48,56; Welland Canal By-Pass 49; Welland Canal Company 47; Welland Raceway 50; Welland Railway 58; Welland Ship Canal 47; Whirlpool Rapids Bridge 68; William B. Rankine Generating Station 63.

3. Local Names

(Businesses, Cemeteries, Churches, Clubs, Conservation Areas, Cultural Groups, Hospitals, Indian Nations, Industries, Libraries, Public Parks, Recreational Localities, Schools, Social Organizations, Stately Homes and Universities.

Albright Gardens 42; Algoma Steel 88; All Saints Church 89; Alfred (home) 92; Alphie's Trough 91; Andrés Wines 87; Anglican Churches 89; Aquinas Catholic High School 93; Armenian Churches, Clubs and Names 44,89; Arthur Bishop House 92; Arthur Schmon Tower 92; Atlas Steel 87,88; Balls Falls Conservation Area 19,95; Barnes Winery 64,87; Barnesdale 64; Bath House 41; Battlefield School 92; Beacon Motor Inn 65; Beamsville Secondary School 92; Bertie Boating Club and Brethren in Christ Church 34; Bishop Ridley College of Ontario 92; Bishop Tonos High School 93; Black Walnut Building 92; Brights Wines 87; Brock University 83,91; Brock's Monument 35; Burch's Mills 40; Burleigh Hill School 92; Burning Spring 40; Butler's Rangers 9,33,35,37,96; Caistor Community Centre 34; Canadian Chautauqua 63; Canadian Martyrs School 92; Canadians Know Their Beer 94; Canby's Mills 40; Carbide Willson 88; Carillon Tower 68; Carleton School 92; Casa Dante 89; Cataract House 41; Cat Nation 23; Cave Spring Cellars 87; Cayuga Indians 23; Celtic Clubs 89; Centennial Hospital Wing 91; Champlain (School) 27,93; Chaplin's 64; Charles Daly Park 94; Château des Charmes Wines 87; Château-Gai Wines 87; Chippawa Creek Conservation Area 95; Chippewa Indians, and variants 23; Christ (Anglican) Church

4. Physical Features

(Climate, Drainage, Lakes, Rivers, Topography and Vegetation)

5. Roads

(Hiking Trails, Rural Roads, Urban Streets, Regional Highways, Scenic Parkways and Provincial Routes).

Abbey 70,77; Aberdeen 75; Academy 72; Achilles 75; Adams 40,77; Addison 63; Aintree 76; Airline 58; Ajax 75; Albert 53,70; Alexandra 74; Algoma 88; Allan 78; Almond 76; Ambrose 53; Anderson 77; Anger 75; Aqueduct 49; Armoury 72; Ash, Ashland, and Ashwood 70,76; Atlas 88; Auditorium 63; Avenue 70; Avenues (route) 78; Ball 75,76; Balsam 76; Barry 78; Bartlett 75; Beacon 65; Beam 43; Beatty 79; Beaver Dams (Beaverdams) 40,72; Beech, and Beechwood 76; Belfast 63; Bell 78; Belton 78; Bennett 75; Bertie Bay 67; Bessey 75; Bidwell 76; Birch, and Birchwood 76; Bishop 75; Bond 74; Booth 76; Bossert 43; Boulevard 70; Boyle 70; Bradley 50,70,74; Brant 25; Brewery 72; Bridge 64,72; Brock 74; Brown 79; Bruce Trail 15; Buchanan 77,78; Bunting 70,77; Burleigh Hill 74,78; Butternut 76; Buttrey 78; Byron 74,76; Caistorville 67; Calais 76; Calvin 52; Cambridge 63,67,76; Cameron 78; Campbell 75,77; Canal and Canal Bank 72; Canboro(ugh) 51,72; Capri 75; Carbide Willson 88; Cardiff 74; Caribou 25; Carlisle 77; Carleton 50,70,74; Carrying Place 34; Carter 77; Case 67; Castlereagh 74,76; Cataract 72; Catharine 53; Catherine 42,70; Cave Spring 72; Cedar 76; Centre 72,75; Champlain 28; Chantal 76; Chapin 76; Charles 74; Charlotte 74; Chartwell 75; Cherry, and Cherrywood 18,76; Chestnut 76; Chippawa Creek Road, and Parkway 72; Christie 74,75; Christmas 77; Church 10,70,72; Churchill 75,76; Circle 70; Citation 76; Clare 78; Clarence 74; Clark 78; Claus 42,75; Colborne 74; College 72; Collier 74; Collingwood 76; Commando 76; Concession Roads 78,79; Concord 18; Coronation 74; Corvette 76; Couke 79; Court 70,77; Coventry 74,76; Crescent 70; Crescent Beach 67; Crook 78; Cross 77; Crown 74; Culp 42,75; Cummington 76; Currie 77; Daley 77; Damude 79; Dauphine 76; Davey 75; David 75; Davis 78; DeCew 44,75,78; Delater 76; Delaware 76; Detenbeck 43; Deverardo 18,77; Dieppe 76; Diltz 51; Disher 75; Dittrick 40; Division 58; Dixon 78; Dobrindt 42,75; Dominion 67; Dorchester 35,72,74; Douglas 78; Dover 76; Drake 78; Drive 70; Drummond 72,74; Dufferin 78; Duke 74; Dunkirk 75,76; Dunn 78; Durham 74,75; Dutch 42; Dwyer 77; East, East Main and Eastwood 53,72,76; Eastman 79; Edelheim 42,75; Edenwood 76; Effingham 72; Eighth 70,72; Elberta 18; Elgin 72; Elizabeth 74; Elm, and Elmwood 18,76; Emerick 78; Epsom 76; Epworth 62; Erie 72; Eton 76; Exeter 75; Export 78; Facer 40,64,68,83; Feeder 72; Fell 75; Ferry 64,68,72,74,76; Fessenden 79; Fielden 78; Fifth 70,79; Fir 76; Firelanes 79; First 70,78,79; Flanagan 67; Fleet 76; Fly 68; Forest 78; Forks 19; Fourth 64,70,78,79; Frank 77; Franklin 77; Fretz 42; Front 51,72,74,75; Frontenac 27; Fuller 77; Gage 74,75; Galaxy 76; Gardiner Place 80; Gate 75; Geneva 70,77; George 78; Gertrude 75; Gibson 77; Glen, Glendale,Glengary, Glengowan, Glenny, Glenridge,and Glenwood 41,70,74,76,78,81,83; Gomorrah 44; Grand 63; Grant 53; Grantham 70; Great Western 58; Green 10,40,76,78,86; Green Boughs 76; Griffin 39; Grouse 76; Grove 76; Gzowski 79; Haig 83; Haight 75; Hainer 40; Haldimand 74; Haney 79; Harcove 78; Harriet 75; Harvard 76; Hartzel 74,75; Hastings 50; Hazel, and Hazelwood 76; Head 50,74; Heights 70; Helliwell 75; Hemlock 76; Hennepin 27; Henrietta 53; Henry 53; Heritage Highway 67; Hiawatha 25; Hickory 76; High 70; Hillside 72; Hodgson 76; Hog 58; Holloway Bay 67; Holmes 75; Hurricane 18; Indian Line 23; Iroquois Trail 21; Isabel 78; Jackson 78; James 77; Jarvis 60; Jasmin 86; Jellicoe 75; John 74,75,78; Johnson 74,75; Jubilee 74; Jupiter 76; Kalar 70; Keating 77; Keats 70; Keefer 52; Kennedy 78; Kentucky 76; Ker 76; Killaly 53; King 10,21,74,75; King's Highway 34; Kinnear 78; Lafayette 76; Lake, Lakeport, Lake Shore, Lakeshore, Lakeview and Lakewood 21,51,64,70,72,74,76; Lancaster 74; Landmarks of Progression 70; Lane 70; Laporte 76; La Salle 27,76; Laval 76; Lawrence 78; Lewis 78; Lexington 76; Lincoln 53,63; Line 1,2,3 78; Linwell 70,83; Lochinvar 78; Lock 50,70,72; Lockhart 76,77; Locust 18; Louis 77; Louth 78; Lundy's 9,38,40,67,72,74; Luther 63; Lybster 88; Lyons Creek Parkway 72; MacDonald-Cartier Freeway 65; Macklem 76; Main 10,21,34,36,53,64,70,74,83,96; Maple, and Maplewood 18,76; Maple Leaf 88; Marc 76; Margarette 78; Marlatts 48; Marlin 78; Marquis 77; Marr 67; Marren 77; Mars 76; Martindale 75,83; Mary 75; Masefield 70; Masterson 78; McArthur 76; McCordick 77; McCormick 76; McGill 76; McGuire 77; McKinnon 88; McLeod 72; McNicholl 77; McQuesten 79; McRae 78; Melba 78; Melville 76; Mercury 76; Merritt, Merritt Trail (Merrittrail) and Merrittville 52,53,70,72,74; Michigan 58; Middle 65,78; Mill 72; Miller 43,67; Mitchell 78; Moffat 77; Mohawk

Trail 21,25; Montrose 72; Morningstar 43; Mountain 15,72,74; Mount Forest 76; Moyer 42,67; Muir 70,79; Murray 74,78; Navy 76; Neff 51; Nello 78; Nelson 76; Neptune 76; Nestor 76; Netherby 72; New Niagara Falls Highway 65; New Portage 34; Newton 75; New York State Thruway (I-90) 65; Niagara 70, 72; Niagara Boulevard 67; Niagara Portage 23,26,34; Niagara River Parkway 26,67,68,72; Niagara Stone 20,67,72; Nickel 88; Ninth 70; Norris 77; North, Northcliff, Northdale, Northglen, Northridge and North Service 65,72; Norton 88; Numbered Roads 21,65,67,70,78,79; Nursery 18; Nye 43; Oak, Oakdale and Oakwood 18,76,83; Oblate 72; Oille 76; Old Garrison 67; Old Portage 34; Omer 78; Ontario 67,70,72; Orchard 10; Ormond 74; Ort 43; Oxford 76; Ozark 25; Packard 88; Paddock Trail 76; Pafford 76; Page 75; Park 63,72,77; Pawling 70,75; Peach 18,76; Pelham 72; Permilla 53; Petrie 77; Pheasant 76; Phelps 52,77; Philip 74; Phipps 78; Picton 74,76; Pilkington 88; Pine, and Pinecrest 76; Place 70; Platoff 74,76; Pluto 76; Plymouth 74,88; Point Abino 67; Portage 25,34,72,74; Post 76; Power Line 72; Preakness 76; Prideaux 74,75; Prince, and Princess 74; Prospect Point 67; Prudhomme 65; Pump House 72; Quarry 72; Queen 10,64,70,74,75; Queens Circle 63; Queen Elizabeth Way (QEW), and variants 65,69,96; Queenston 21,72,74; Race 50; Railroad, and Railway 58; Rebecca 53; Rebstock 63; Regent 74,75; REO 88; Ricardo 74; Richmond 76; Ridge, Ridgemount, Ridgeway and Ridgewood 15,76,82; Riordan 77; Rittenhouse 39; River, and Riverview 72; Road Through the Settlements 34; Robbie Burns 75; Robert 78; Robert Moses Parkway 67; Robinson 78; Roosevelt 76,78; Rosewood 76; Rye 76; Ryerson 62; Rykert 77; Rysdale 76; St. Catharines 72; St. Catharines and Merritsville Turnpike 72; St. David ('s) 72; St. Joseph 72; St. Paul 21,74,77,89; Salina 72; Sauer 75; Sawmilll 10; Scenic Drive 67; School 72; Schwalm 77; Scott 64,70,75,78; Second 70,78,79; Secord 35; Seventh 70,79; SG2-SG21 79; Shannon 63; Shawnee 25; Shawninigan 88; Shelley 70; Sherk 43; Sherkston Beach 95; Shickluna 53; Sider 67; Simcoe 74,75; Singer 79; Sixth 70,79; Smith 67; Sodom 44; Solar 76; South 72; Sovereign 78; Springbank 62; Spruce 76; Stanley 64,72,78; Station 72; Steele 78; Strathmore 78; Streets (Louth) 78; Sugarloaf Hill 72; Sulphur Springs 72; Swamp 20; Swan 77; Swansea 74; Swayze 79; Sylvan 76 Talbot Trail 67; Tanguay 76; Tecumseh 25; Temple 63; Tennessee 62; Terrace 70; Third 70,78,79; Thole 76; Thomas 77; Thorold Stone 67,72; Townline 67,72,78; Towpath 51; Trafalgar 75; Tufford 42; Tunis 75; Turney 79; Union 88; Valencia 75; Valentino 75; Valley, and Valleyview 72; Vanier 76; Varsity 76; Verdun 75; Via Dell Monte 75; Victoria 53,64,67,72,74,75,78; Victory 76; Vincent 63; Vine 70,78; Vineland 67 Vittoria 53; Wabasso 88; Walnut 76; Watson 76; Weaver 43; Wedsworth 76; Weinbrenner 43; Welland 70; Wellington 74,76; Wesley 63; West, Westchester, West Main and Westwood 53,72,76; Whirlpool 17; Wilberforce 63; Wilkes 77; William 75; Willick 43; Willow, and Willowood 76; Willo-Dell 78; Willson 79,88; Windmill Point 67,72; Winery 64; Winger 43; Winston 75; Winter 75; Wood, Woodbine, Woodfield, Woodgate and Woodington 76; Woodruff 77; Wright 77 Wycliffe 63; Wynn 75; Yale 76; Yates 52-53; Youngblut 78; Zimmerman 40; Zion 67.

6. Ships' Names

(Canal, Lake and River Vessels and Shipping Companies, yesterday and today)

"A" Vessels 56; Acorn 56; Advance 56; Akranes 56; Alexander 56; Algocen 55; Algoma Central Railway 55,87; Algorail 55; Algosoo 55; Algoway 55; Americana 57; Ann(ie) and Jane 56; Arctic 56; Asia 56; Ayr 56; Bridge-It 57; Brock 56; Canada Steamship Lines 87; Canadiana 57; Canadian Century 55,56; Canadian Olympic 56; Canadian Progress 55,56; Cape Breton Miner 55; Cayuga 57; Chicora 57; Chippewa 57; Cibola 57; Clifton 56; Corona 57; Dalhousie City 57; Dove 57; Eglantine 56; Empress of India 56; Enterprise 56; Garden City 57; Gazelle 57; Gordon C. Leitch 55; Hamilton 56; H.M.C.S. Fort Erie, Humberstone, Merrittonia, Niagara, Port Colborne, St. Catharines and Thorlock 57; H.M. Griffiths 56; Imperial Acadia 55; International Steam Bridge 57; James Norris

Photocredits

ABOUT THE AUTHOR

Dr. John N. Jackson is Professor of Applied Geography at Brock University. His interests are in the history and character of cities in Canada and Western Europe. He began his career in Britain and moved to Canada in 1961, first of the West Coast and then to the Niagara Region in 1965, where his studies have included recreational, industrial and urban aspects of the landscape. His travels and urban experiences extend to Australia, New Zealand, Russia and China. He is married with three children.